Jeremiah: Spokesman Out of Time

Jeremiah
SPOKESMAN OUT OF TIME

William L. Holladay

A PILGRIM PRESS BOOK
from United Church Press, Philadelphia

Copyright © 1974 United Church Press
All Rights Reserved

No part of this publication may be reproduced, stored in a retrieval system, or transmitted in any form or by any means, electronic, mechanical, photocopying, recording, or otherwise, without the prior permission of the publisher.

Library of congress Cataloging in Publication Data

Holladay, William Lee.
    Jeremiah: spokesman out of time.

    "A Pilgrim Press book."
    Bibliography: p.
    1. Bible. O.T. Jeremiah—Criticism, interpretation, etc. 2. Jeremiah, the prophet. I. Title.
    BS1525.2.H64   224'.2'07   74-7052
    ISBN 0-8298-0283-5

The scripture quotations in this publication are (unless otherwise indicated) from the *Revised Standard Version of the Bible,* copyrighted © 1946 and 1952 by the Division of Christian Education, National Council of Churches, and are used by permission.

The Pilgrim Press, 132 West 31 Street
New York, New York 10001

Contents

Foreword

This book has been taking shape in my mind for more than a dozen years, as I have been involved in various churches with adult classes on the prophet Jeremiah. These classes, as one might imagine, have been meant for folk who are not specialists in biblical studies but who have wanted to enlarge their understanding of the story of God's ways with his people.

I have made every effort in this study to keep the presentation straightforward and clear; whether I have succeeded is another matter. Readers will find, I fear, that the material often betrays that habit of the professor: the raising of questions. There may be more questions here, more doubts, more uncertainties than many readers will feel comfortable with—particularly in the last chapter, where I try to give a fair presentation of what the story of Jeremiah can mean to us today. I can only say that to my mind the raising of questions about scripture is not a wicked thing to do; indeed, scripture itself implies questions as the careful reader begins to notice contrasts, differences of perspective, and other curiosities within its pages. Many generations within the Jewish and Christian communities have raised such questions; in the meantime, scripture has survived—and thrived. And it will survive and thrive on our questions too. As we raise our own questions and discover our own answers, our eyes will be sharpened and the biblical story will emerge in clearer focus for us.

There may be another difficulty in this material: there will inevitably be, in the course of the story, something about those old battles and wars and kings with hard names. But if we are going to bring Jeremiah to life again in the mind's eye, it will be worth our effort not to skip the hard names. The point is, real people running real governments were having real problems in those days, as people have had since. We must take a bit of trouble to see what the headlines were all about. Otherwise, if we are vague about the headlines, Jeremiah will probably remain for us a distant figure in a stained-glass window. I shall promise to give the hard names gradually, and not all at once.

I also urge on the reader that this book not be taken as a substitute for the reading and studying of the Old Testament book of Jeremiah, but rather as a companion to it. I shall not be quoting all the relevant Old Testament material; usually I shall simply offer comment on the text and give some of the background and illustrative material which I hope will illuminate the text. But a chapter-and-verse citation should be looked up, and read, when it appears. (When a phrase or a passage is quoted in this study, it is normally from the *Revised Standard Version.*) Incidentally, for simplicity's sake all references to a chapter (or chapter and verse) in Arabic numerals, unaccompanied by any book reference, are to be understood as citations to a particular passage of the book of Jeremiah (and of course to the English verse references rather than to the Hebrew ones, when these differ). Cross-references to other chapters *within this present study* are in Roman numerals.

One more point. Various scholars will differ to some degree in their reconstruction of many matters connected with the book of Jeremiah: their understanding of the way the book took shape, their conviction about the degree to which the present text of the book does or does not represent what Jeremiah actually said or did on a given occasion, their understanding of Jeremiah's conception of his own mission, and their solution to various problems of chronology. These matters, which are fought out in the technical journals and commentaries, often have important consequences in the total portrait of Jeremiah which they present to the world at large. And because my own studies in the book of Jeremiah, pursued off and on for the last couple of decades, have convinced me that some of the conclusions in the commentaries should be amended, I have had occasion to publish from time to time these new suggestions of mine. (See Additional Reading and Resources at the end of the book.) Some of these suggestions are embodied in the present work, though of course in less technical form, but it is only fair to warn the reader that not all scholars would agree with everything presented here. I have tried my best, however, to be responsible in my presentation.

I should like to express my thanks to all those thoughtful folk through the years—in the Chicago area in 1960-1963, in Beirut, Lebanon, in 1963-1970, and in New England since 1970—who have had a hand in this book by teaching me through their questions and their responses what is really important in the book of Jeremiah. In particular, thanks to members of the Near East Mission of the United Church Board for World Ministries, who invited me to lead them in the study of Jeremiah at their biennial meeting in Istanbul, Turkey, in the spring of 1966, and who thereby forced me for the first time to try to write down in nontechnical form what seems crucial about Jeremiah.[1]

This study is offered, then, to church and classroom in the hope that it can stimulate discussion and further exploration, not only of Jeremiah but of other portions of scripture as well. Pastor John Robinson's parting words to the Pilgrim Fathers in 1620 are appropriate here; a friend recalled, "For he was very confident the Lord had more truth and light yet to break forth out of his holy Word."[2]

Chapter I

The World of Jeremiah

The prophet Jeremiah is an exceptional figure in the biblical record, both in the extent of his own words which are recorded and in the extent of the biographical information recorded about him. His own words—mostly "oracles" (that is, short poetic units announcing God's judgment or his restoration) but also some sermons as well—appear mostly in chapters 2 through 23 or so, and in chapters 30-31 and some of chapters 46-51. The biographical information about him appears mostly in chapters 26-29 and 32-44. We have more biographical information about King David in the Old Testament, and more recorded words from the apostle Paul in the New; but in the extent of both recorded words and biographical information in the Bible, Jeremiah would be difficult to match.

We not only know a very great deal of his words and deeds; his words and deeds give every evidence for his being a highly original sort of person who appeared at a turning point in the history of the people of the Old Testament. That turning point was the fall of Jerusalem, the capital of the kingdom of Judah, to Nebuchadnezzar, the king of the great empire of Babylon, in 587 B.C. Jeremiah's ministry was lived out in the last few decades of that kingdom of Judah, and for at least a year or two after the fall of Jerusalem. He was convinced that his mission was to announce to his people the judgment of God upon them for their disloyalty. He envisaged this judgment primarily in the shape of a victory of the Babylonian army. And because the Babylonian army did

11

invade, and Judah did fall, Jeremiah was largely responsible for shaping a theology adequate for the disaster which overwhelmed the people; and because there was no alternative theology available which had the adequacy that Jeremiah's did, it was his outlook which helped to shape the people's view of itself for those terrible years of defeat and humiliation and, indeed, for the half century following his death when the people were forced to reconceive their destiny through and through.

All this should suffice to alert us to his importance, since we ourselves are witnesses in the twentieth century both to triumph and to disaster in human fortune which seem to us almost unmatched.

But there is even more to Jeremiah which attracts many in our own generation to him. Alone of the "prophets" of the Old Testament, he saw his relationship with God to be a problem to be grappled with, more than an obligation simply to be taken for granted. There had been other spokesmen for God, great ones, in times past—Elijah and Amos, Hosea and Micah and Isaiah—but one finds, in reading through the pages that record their words and deeds, that once they became convinced that God was calling them to speak, they spoke, and that was that; no question (so far as our record goes) crossed their minds regarding the process of their being called. But Jeremiah, while he went ahead and spoke, still hesitated before accepting the task and continued constantly to question the way God was treating him. In his capacity (and willingness) to question and to doubt, he stands apart from the rest of the array of folk whom we meet in the pages of scripture, and this capacity (and willingness) brings him close to us. For while there are many in our day who are willing to undertake a life of faith lived under God's guidance and care, there are few who do not at some point question his ways, or wish they dared to.

We must begin by taking some account of the world in which Jeremiah grew up and lived his life. For a point of time, we shall say 627 B.C.; and for locale, of course, we turn to Palestine.

Now Palestine is a geographical term, not a political one; it refers to the area at the eastern end of the Mediterranean Sea where the people of the Old Testament lived out their destiny and their faith. It is a surprisingly small area, really not much larger in extent than the state of New Hampshire or the state of

Vermont (about ten thousand square miles). Within this area are several spots suitable for large-scale farming, notably on the coast and in the valley of Jezreel (Esdraelon) in the north, but most of the region is cut up by hills and dry stream beds (very much like the arroyos of the American Southwest), made suitable for agriculture only by the patient terracing of hillsides. Those who are familiar with the way the land looks east of Santa Barbara or San Diego can form some idea of the terrain, though those areas of California receive less rainfall than Palestine does.

Palestine may receive more rain than does southern California, but the pattern of rainy and dry seasons is much the same: the rainy season begins late in October and continues off and on until March or April, and the dry season lasts through the summer and early fall. The amount of rain varies from north to south and from west to east, the areas in the north and west getting the most; little rain reaches beyond the hills west of the Jordan River. Jerusalem receives about 24 inches of rain per year.

Into this area, a "land bridge" between Egypt and the great civilizations of the east (Assyria and Babylonia), there came, in the course of the thirteenth century B.C., a people with a fresh sense of community, the people called Israel. Their sense of community was shaped by a new vision, a new understanding of God. They were convinced that God had appeared to Moses, had revealed to Moses the name by which the people were to know him (Yahweh), and had then "covenanted" or contracted with them, under the guidance of Moses; this covenanting, or contracting, had taken place at the mountain of Sinai. The covenant bound Yahweh and Israel together; Israel was to be "his people" and Yahweh was to be "their God." He for his part would protect them in war and prosper them in peace, and the people for their part were to be an experimental community, regulating their lives by mutual support and a concern for the helpless and continuing to be sensitive to God's will. For many decades this people worked out the patterns of their common life on the basis of these traditions from Sinai and reaffirmed their mutual loyalty to Yahweh at religious centers like Shiloh, where the Ark of the Covenant was kept—evidently a kind of box or chest which represented the presence of Yahweh with them.

But new pressures came in the course of time, principally the military threat of the Philistines, another group of people along

13

the southern coast; and Israel found herself late in the eleventh century B.C. forced to set up the institution of kingship for the sake of tighter and more secure government. This kingship began with Saul and prospered under David and Solomon but then broke in two, north and south, because of regional pressures. It is true that the people never lost their sense of united "peoplehood" under Yahweh, but thereafter they were to be two kingdoms politically: a northern kingdom, called Israel (confusingly, for us, since that term was also applied to the totality of the people, north and south), which finally settled on a capital at Samaria; and a southern kingdom, called Judah, which held onto the Jerusalem of David and Solomon for its capital. We have already said that all of Palestine is roughly the size of New Hampshire; Judah, very much the smaller of the two kingdoms, was scarcely larger than the present state of Rhode Island—and our story will center on Judah.

Before we turn to Judah, however, we must take account of the empire of Assyria. Assyria had its capital at various locations on the upper Tigris River, far to the east of Palestine; the final one— Nineveh—was located where the city of Mosul, in northern Iraq, is today. As the crow flies, it is about six hundred miles north and east of Jerusalem. Its armies were the horror of the Middle East; for several hundred years they had spread outward from the center of the empire to all points of the compass, killing and burning, ruling by deportation and terror. Perhaps not until the coming of the Mongols (in the thirteenth century A.D.) would the people of the area so greatly fear and hate another conqueror. (We can have a glimpse of the hatred which the Jews held for the Assyrians by reading the gloating account which they framed when Nineveh finally, finally was falling; it is found in the book of Nahum, 1:12—3:19.)

A hundred years before the time of Jeremiah, the Assyrians had marched into Palestine and besieged the capital of the northern kingdom, Samaria, until it fell; Isaiah, a prophet in Jerusalem at the time, warned his people from a distance about what was happening. Two decades later the Assyrians returned and marched to the very gates of Jerusalem; this time Isaiah watched the siege with his own eyes. After some time, to the surprise of most people but to the fulfillment of Isaiah's assurances, the Assyrian army suddenly pulled up stakes and

14

marched home again. But the hot breath of the Assyrian empire was heavy on Judah in the years that followed. The long reign of King Manasseh of Judah (687-642 B.C.) was one frantic attempt to save the nation intact, to assure its survival on any terms; and Judah did survive, barely, by becoming a puppet kingdom, a satellite of Assyria, by sending heavy tribute ("protection money," we would say) year by year to Assyria, by erecting Assyrian altars in the Temple area of Jerusalem, by cultivating astrology and fortune-telling in the Assyrian fashion—anything to assure Assyria of her loyalty, anything to survive.

Then, after King Manasseh's death and after the two-year reign of his son, Amon, the boy king Josiah came to the throne. By the time Josiah had become an adult it was plain that he was a great deal more sensitive religiously than his grandfather Manasseh had been. And something else was plain, too, by the year 627 B.C., when we begin our story: Assyria was growing weaker. This news was the best news anyone had heard in a long time. The feeling was in the air that Assyria was starting to rot from within, that her policy of ruling by terror was beginning to be counterproductive, as political people say today, that it was beginning to be safe for her subject peoples to show a little independence from her. In short, people sensed that new policies were possible. (And it was true; by 612 B.C. Assyrian power would shrink to nothing, for she would be defeated by her southern rival, Babylonia. No one knew the time would come when Babylonia would simply take over Assyria's imperial designs, alas, and pursue them with equal vigor.)

It was in this period, when the foundations of international life were being shaken, that Jeremiah was growing up.

We have said nothing in detail about the religious convictions of the Israelites, about what they believed about creation and redemption and human destiny; and we have said nothing, either, about the way they organized their religious observance. Some of these matters will be referred to, as there is need, in the course of our exploration of the words and deeds of Jeremiah. Because we must plunge into our central concern. And so we turn to chapter 1 of the book of Jeremiah, which records his perception of being called by God to speak out.

Chapter II

The Prophet Like Moses

Chapter 1 of the book of Jeremiah opens with three verses of a kind of editorial note, placed there so that any reader can know the immediate situation of Jeremiah's career.

To those who lived nearer the times and places of the events, verse 1 is heavy with details which set the stage. "The words of Jeremiah, the son of Hilkiah, of the priests who were in Anathoth in the land of Benjamin. . . ." The site of Anathoth, Jeremiah's village, is just three miles northeast of Jerusalem; the spot is a rocky prominence that the local Arabs today call "the summit of the carob beans." Memories are long in the Middle East, and the present-day Arab village just north of this spot carries the same name as that of Jeremiah's village: in Arabic, 'Anata. From that hillock where Jeremiah grew up, one may clearly see the walls of Jerusalem; the lad grew up, then, not *in* the great capital city but within sight of it. His father, Hilkiah, was a priest and so would have presided at the sacrifices of the villagers at Anathoth. (This was before the days of King Josiah's great reform, after which no sacrifices would be allowed other than those at the Temple in Jerusalem. We shall discuss this reform presently.)

The priests had another function in those days, too: they had the responsibility of preserving and handing on the old traditions of instruction in covenant norms—how the community of Israel was expected to behave in the sight of God. This instruction was called *tōrāh:* not quite "law" in our sense (that would be a development of later times) but teaching, instruction in the

16

stipulations that God had made to Israel about the conduct of life. The priests, then, were charged with the responsibility for the old testimony of Israel.

And there may have been a very special set of memories at Anathoth, the memories that had belonged to Shiloh, though of this we cannot be absolutely sure. Centuries before, when the Ark of the Covenant (that symbol of the presence of God) was kept at the sanctuary at Shiloh, twenty miles north of Anathoth, there was a priest named Eli who officiated at the sanctuary there, who watched the boy Samuel grow up with him. It is just possible that Jeremiah absorbed from his father the traditions about Samuel at Shiloh; what is certain is that Shiloh and Samuel entered into Jeremiah's thinking. The link between Shiloh and Anathoth may be this: King Solomon bade the priest Abiathar retire to Anathoth after he had been deposed (1 Kings 2:26), and that same Abiathar is reported to have been the last survivor of the house of Eli the priest.[1] And of course if Anathoth was the repository for the old traditions of Shiloh, then to an even greater degree it would be a repository for the far older traditions of Moses, for the Ark of the Covenant, kept at Shiloh, had been in the vanguard of Israel's wilderness wanderings when Moses had led them to freedom and to covenant obedience.[2] No wonder, then, that when Jeremiah at one point in his career contemplated the intercessory task he had before the people, the two earlier figures that leaped to his mind were Moses and Samuel (15:1).

The second verse of the chapter gives us an important clue on chronology: "to whom the word of the Lord came in the days of Josiah the son of Amon, king of Judah, in the thirteenth year of his reign." Josiah we have met. Data elsewhere in the Old Testament indicate that he took the throne in 640 B.C., so that the thirteenth year of his reign would be 627 B.C.: this is the reference year for our description of the historical situation which we have already mentioned several times. Now what precisely happened to Jeremiah in 627 B.C.? To decide, we must have a preliminary look at the description that has come down to us of the call of Jeremiah (verses 4-10).

> Now the word of the Lord came to me saying,
> "Before I formed you in the womb I knew you,
> and before you were born I consecrated you;

17

I appointed you a prophet to the nations."
Then I said, "Ah, Lord God! Behold, I do not know how to
speak, for I am only a youth." But the Lord said to me,
"Do not say, 'I am only a youth';
for to all to whom I send you you shall go,
and whatever I command you you shall speak.
Be not afraid of them,
for I am with you to deliver you,
    says the Lord."
Then the Lord put forth his hand and touched my mouth;
and the Lord said to me,
"Behold, I have put my words in your mouth.
See, I have set you this day over nations and over kingdoms,
to pluck up and to break down,
to destroy and to overthrow,
to build and to plant."

Here is a portrayal of a reluctant prophet. God, we are told,
called Jeremiah, and Jeremiah tried to beg off; but God overruled
his hesitation and assured him that he would be protected by God
in all that he undertook on God's behalf. We shall return in a
moment to discuss the matter of Jeremiah's hesitation, but first
we must try to settle the matter of chronology. Chronological
discussions may at the outset seem tedious, but this one is
necessary for our question, to put Jeremiah into focus.

Now commentators have almost unanimously assumed, and
without question, that 627 B.C. is the date for the beginning of
Jeremiah's career as a prophet; in this view, he began to speak
out God's words to his fellow citizens in that year.[3] But there are
three major difficulties with this view: (1) we find no oracles of
Jeremiah which can be assigned with any confidence to the time
of Josiah's reign; (2) in particular, there is no word from Jeremiah
about the great reform of King Josiah in 621 B.C., and (3) there is
no good candidate in that period of time for the "foe from the
north" about whom Jeremiah constantly spoke (1:14-16, 4:5-8,
and often). These difficulties in the traditional chronology force
upon us what I think is a very simple solution which brings with it
a much clearer and more plausible picture of Jeremiah's self-
understanding than we had had. Let us then take up these difficulties one by one.

18

1. We find no oracles of Jeremiah which can confidently be assigned to the time of Josiah's reign. This is negative evidence, admittedly, but the matter is still worrisome. The conventional view of Josiah was that he was a good and excellent king, beyond compare (2 Kings 23:25), and while Jeremiah could conceivably have differed to some degree from this judgment, the single reference which we have from him about Josiah is thoroughly positive (22:15-16, a passage which offers Jeremiah's negative judgment of King Jehoiakim in comparison with his father, Josiah). Now we cannot assume that the oracles in the early chapters of Jeremiah (that is, chapters 2-10) were necessarily the earliest to be delivered in Jeremiah's career, but the chances are that they were. And the main thrust of these oracles, as we shall see in chapter III, is that Israel has gone quite radically astray, has broken the covenant with God, has been "harlotrous" with fertility deities, and that consequently God is about to launch a fearful enemy from the north to lay waste and destroy the land and people. This overwhelmingly bleak picture simply does not seem to fit the situation of King Josiah's time. Josiah had hopes to reestablish his sovereignty over the lost territories of the north; according to 2 Chronicles 34 he began a religious-political reform as early as his twelfth year (thus the year before our date of 627!), smashing the (presumably pagan) altars in the north (2 Chronicles 34:3-7). And, as we shall see in a moment, he undertook a quite thoroughgoing reform in Jerusalem in 621. Further, we may go on to affirm that there are no oracles elsewhere in the book of Jeremiah which seem to fit the circumstances of these years either. All of the presumably early oracles of Jeremiah fit the historical situation of the reign of Jehoiakim, the son of Josiah, far better. Finally, there is no oracle from Jeremiah's lips regarding the death of Josiah. The king's death was a sudden and quite unexpected event for the people— he was struck down in the prime of life in 609 B.C. (when he was thirty-nine years old), in an unfortunate battle at Megiddo; we shall have more to say about this battle presently. This death, I repeat, sent a shock wave through the sensibilities of the populace.[4] But again, not a trace of this stunning event is to be found in the words of Jeremiah. In short, nothing that we know from the time of King Josiah seems to fit anything we can learn from the book of Jeremiah.

2. In particular, there is no word from Jeremiah about the reform of King Josiah in 621 B.C. This matter might well have been discussed under (1), but it is so important in itself as to require special attention. The reform of which we speak is described in detail in 2 Kings 22:3—23:24. Josiah sponsored the renovation of the Temple facilities, and a scroll was discovered which purported to be the words of Moses to Israel; scholars now believe that the description found in 2 Kings of that scroll fits best the book of Deuteronomy, or at least the core (perhaps chapters 12-26) of the book of Deuteronomy, so that it is altogether likely that the occasion of the discovery of the scroll was the time when the book of Deuteronomy first came into public view. The king, according to the account, was abashed at how far the public practice of religion had drifted from what the scroll enjoined; he found a prophetess who could certify the authenticity of the scroll, and he then had it read publicly and saw to it that the citizenry undertook to carry out its injunctions. He sponsored a total public reform on the basis of the various instructions of the scroll: all the claptrap of fertility cult worship was pulled down from the Temple area; all the personnel of fertility cult worship and of the various astrological cults were turned out. Further, all religious observances (that is, sacrifices) in areas outside of Jerusalem were forbidden, and the priests of those centers were organized to take their turn instead at sacrifice in Jerusalem; the festival of the Passover was reinstituted (the narrator says, after a lapse of four hundred years—2 Kings 23:22), and there was in general an enormous bustle of public piety. One wonders whether there was not political gain as well as religious virtue to be gar- nered from this reform; one recent authority suspects that the king's motive was at least partly to obtain an increase of tax receipts for Jerusalem.[5] But never mind, it was a reform; no change in public religious practice as thoroughgoing had been made since Solomon's Temple was built. And of this event, what did Jeremiah think? There is not a trace of reaction, either positive or negative. A few scholars have wondered whether the appeal to adhere to "this covenant" which is found in 11:1-13 might not refer to the reform, but most scholars think the wording in that passage is too vague and that the phrase "this covenant" means what the context says it means—the covenant at

20

Sinai mediated by Moses (verse 4). Curious, this silence on Jeremiah's part.

3. There is no good candidate in this period for the "foe from the north" about whom Jeremiah speaks so often. The Assyrians had stopped marching west; their successors the Babylonians were not yet marching west—that would come later. Scholars were pressed some decades ago to solve the puzzle by assuming that Jeremiah was speaking of the Scythians, a nomadic group from the far north (southern Russia) who, according to a report of the Greek historian Herodotus, invaded the Palestinian coast during those days.[6] But more recently scholars have abandoned this solution: there is no record in the Old Testament of a Scythian invasion of Palestine, and the description that Jeremiah gives of the foe from the north would in no way fit the Scythians; many authorities these days feel that there is a mythological or "fairy-tale" dimension to Jeremiah's description of the foe. (We shall discuss this problem more fully in chapter IV.)

But these puzzling features of Jeremiah's message are solved if we assume that he began to preach not in 627 B.C. at all but rather during the reign of Jehoiakim, 609-598 B.C. There was evidently a reversion in Jehoiakim's reign to some of the religious practices which King Josiah had outlawed (compare 7:16-18); Jeremiah was steadily at odds with this king and his shortsighted ways (see chapter 36, as well as 22:13-17, a passage we have already noticed). The reform of Josiah was past history and no longer carefully enforced, and everyone could sense who the foe from the north was; it was Babylon (read 2 Kings 24, and compare Jeremiah 5:15-17).

What, then, are we to make of the date 627 B.C., the thirteenth year of Josiah, which we find in 1:2? Is it a mistake? No, I do not think so, and the clue is right in front of us, in 1:5:

> Before I formed you in the womb I knew you,
> and before you were born I consecrated you;
> I appointed you a prophet to the nations.

It was when he was a youth, true, that Jeremiah responded to the call from God, but beyond that he sensed that God had *always* been knocking at the door of his life, even from the time before he

21

was born. I suggest, then, quite simply, that the thirteenth year of Josiah is the date of Jeremiah's *birth,* and that whenever anyone would ask Jeremiah when the word of the Lord had come to him, he would reply, with utter justification, "In the thirteenth year of Josiah," because "Before I formed you in the womb I knew you . . . ." If this assumption is correct, Jeremiah would have been six years old when Josiah instituted his great reform; what excited discussion there must have been in the household for the boy to overhear, when his father Hilkiah learned that he must thereafter take his turn in going to Jerusalem to officiate at sacrifice, all because a scroll with the words of Moses had just been circulated in Jerusalem!

There is one more bit of evidence of a more positive nature to reinforce our suggested chronology, and that is found in 15:16, where Jeremiah is complaining to God that God has not properly looked after him. The first line has some very strange wording: "Thy words were found, and I ate them." Some scholars simply assume that the phrase "thy words were found" refers to the reception of the divine word by the prophet, but others are worried by the phrase, and several scholars prefer to abandon the Hebrew wording altogether and follow the quite different Greek text, which connects verse 16 closely with the end of verse 15: "Know that for thy sake I bear reproach from those who despise thy words. Consume them, and thy word will be the joy and delight of my heart."[7]

But there is no need to abandon the wording of our Hebrew text, which makes perfectly good sense. The only real parallel in the Old Testament for the expression "thy words were found" is to be located in the description of the finding of the scroll in the Temple area, 2 Kings 22:13, 23:2: "the words of the book (of the covenant) which had been found." I suggest, very simply, that the phrase "thy words were found" in 15:16 is a poetic reference to the finding of the scroll in the Temple in 621 B.C., so that "and I ate them" refers to Jeremiah's own acceptance of God's call (similar to "Behold I have put my words in your mouth," spoken by God to Jeremiah in 1:9); thus, by this understanding of 15:16, Jeremiah must have accepted the call *after* the finding of the scroll in 621 B.C. and not before—and thus not in 627 B.C.

By this dating, then, Jeremiah would have been eighteen years old when King Josiah was killed at the battle of Megiddo in 609

22

B.C. We have already mentioned what a shock the king's sudden death was to the nation. Now let us look more closely at the circumstances of that battle. Nineveh, the capital of Assyria, had fallen in 612 B.C. to the rival Babylonians. A complicated three-cornered struggle ensued, because the third power in the Near East was Egypt. Egypt had of course traditionally been the enemy of Assyria; there had been steady rivalry through the centuries as to which empire would control the land between them—that is, Palestine. Now that Assyria had fallen and the remnants of her empire had fled north and west, however, Egypt perceived *Babylonia* to be the new threat, and suddenly tried to come to the *rescue* of Assyria, to maintain the balance of power. Egypt sent an army north, through Palestine; Josiah, still convinced that *Assyria* was the main threat, tried to prevent the passage of the Egyptians on their way to support Assyria; and in this way Josiah met his death. It was a foolish move for the king to make, of course, and events thereafter followed thick and fast. Josiah's son Jehoahaz was crowned king but was able to rule only three months before he was captured by the Egyptians and taken off to Egypt, where he died; and his brother Jehoiakim was then put on the throne as a puppet by the Egyptians. Jehoiakim was to rule eleven years, but the independence of the kingdom of Judah was really over. Four years after he came onto the throne the Babylonians defeated the Egyptians and the remnants of Assyria in an important battle in north Syria, at Carchemish (605 B.C.), and King Jehoiakim thereupon switched sides and became a puppet of the Babylonians; and then again, when he thought it was safe, tried to gain independence from the Babylonians. In short, it was a time of frantic turmoil for Judah. Yesterday's enemies are today's friends. It was not a time for most folk to ponder calmly what God wished of his people. This, then, by the chronology here suggested, was the situation into which the eighteen-year-old Jeremiah was plunged, on the death of King Josiah. It is a chronology which fits the evidence of Jeremiah's first pronouncements. To be sure, if we have secured 627 B.C. as the date of Jeremiah's *birth*, then we have no very secure date for Jeremiah's *acceptance* of his call from God. But it could well have been quite soon after the beginning of the reign of Jehoiakim, in 609 B.C., for the first dated event found in the biographical material on Jeremiah is the delivery of the so-called Temple

23

Sermon, "In the beginning of the reign of Jehoiakim" (26:1). (For our study of the Temple Sermon, see chapter V.)

Now that we have formed our theory of the immediate circumstances of Jeremiah's youth, let us take a closer look at the words of the call itself, as Jeremiah recorded them (1:4-10). What does verse 5 mean? What would it mean to be appointed a "prophet to the nations"?

First we need to get a clearer idea of what the Old Testament understands by the "word of God." The Hebrew expression *dābār*, usually translated in English by "word," also means "thing." This double meaning of *dābār* puzzles students at first, until they begin to realize that for the Israelite "word" and "event" are part of the same perceived experience. What a person thinks and plans, what a person says, what a person does, all are part of the *same* event. Spoken words, then, in the Israelite understanding, have power to change situations fully as much as deeds do, and as powerfully; one has only to think of the deathbed "blessing" of Isaac in Genesis 27, or the "curses" reported elsewhere in the Old Testament (for example, Shimei's curse of King David in 2 Samuel 16:5-13 and the sequel in 1 Kings 2:8-9), to realize how powerful words could be to the Israelite. Look up the law in Leviticus 19:14! And of course when one speaks of *God's* word, it is a word that implies a deed as well, a deed at the time, or again a deed-to-be, a deed in the works. When we read, "And God said, 'Let there be light' (Gen. 1:3)," then there *was* light: just the saying of it does it. The best description of the power of God's word to get things done is found in Isaiah 55:10-11. Read it. What is an "empty word"? An empty word is an echo, which returns without having accomplished anything. But God's word is not like that; it gets things done.

So for the prophet to speak God's word is an awesome thing. It is not just to get up and say, "I suggest that the will of God for our day is thus and so." On the contrary, it is to let loose power for good or ill upon the people; it is as if someone were to smash a flask of deadly bacteria into a crowd—the germs are in the air, they are doing their work, and no one can call them back. The deed is done.

There was, of course, in Israel a long tradition of prophets, spokesmen for God. There was Nathan, who told the king he was wrong to steal Bathsheba from Uriah (2 Samuel 12:7); there was

24

Elijah, who pronounced a drought (1 Kings 17:1) and told the king he was wrong to steal the vineyard from Naboth (1 Kings 21:20); there were Amos and Hosea, Micah and Isaiah, and many more. But what if you feel in your bones that the end is coming upon your people (compare Jeremiah 20:8-9)? What if you feel that all is lost and that God has picked you out to do the telling to your people—what then? If you feel impelled to speak out that Jerusalem is destroyed (compare 26:6, 9), then, though the walls and towers of Jerusalem be for the moment intact, their doom is sealed.

Toward the end of World War II the Germans set aside the castle of Colditz in the eastern part of the country to serve as the prison for Allied officers who had previously been taken prisoner and had then escaped from other prisons and been recaptured by the Germans; Colditz was reputed to be escape-proof and was reserved for the "bad boys." One day in Colditz a British officer was seen planting minute amounts of dry rot into the beams of the castle. He argued with a twinkle in his eye that if the R.A.F. could remove the roof of a building in a second or so, then dry rot could do the same thing, though in a somewhat longer span of time—say, twenty years. Since the war might last that long, he was conceivably doing as much damage to the castle as a fair-sized bomb might.[8]

So with Jerusalem: Jeremiah would, by his very words, be planting the dry rot in the timbers of Jerusalem. Look at 5:14: the word is fire, and burns! No wonder Jeremiah shrank from the task. No wonder, when he did accept the call—when, four years along in Jehoiakim's reign, the king heard a scroll of Jeremiah's words being read—no wonder the king burned the scroll (chapter 36, especially verse 23) as one might burn the mattress of a neighbor who has just died of the plague. The words have done enough damage orally; let them not do further damage in written form![7]

And notice, too, that Jeremiah's call is specifically to the "nations," plural, not simply to Judah alone. There are no limits to God's sovereignty, and so no limits to the scope of Jeremiah's ministry. No wonder Jeremiah hesitates. He is too young, he believes. Now the way in which a potential prophet may have perceived a call from God is far past the reach of all our inquiry; but still, there may have been impulses which helped to prepare the way in which the prophet became aware of his call. So here: I

25

have a suspicion about one factor, at least, which fed into Jeremiah's sense of God's pressing in upon his life, and that is a curious verse in Deuteronomy—18:18. This verse, by our reconstruction, would have been part of that scroll found in the Temple when Jeremiah was a small boy. This verse, as we can see, states that God told Moses that some day, long after Moses, God would raise up another prophet, a prophet like Moses, who would continue the process of announcing God's word to his people. The wording by which Jeremiah perceived God's call—"Behold, I have put my words in your mouth" (1:9), "whatever I command you you shall speak" (1:7)—is very close to the wording of the verse in Deuteronomy that speaks of the prophet like Moses— "I will put my words in his mouth, and he shall speak to them all that I command him (Deut. 18:18)." No other call of a prophet in the Old Testament resembles this verse in Deuteronomy so much. There may be other possible explanations for the closeness of wording, but I think it is easiest to understand it as Jeremiah's conviction that *he* is the prophet like Moses.

After all, the great question in his mind after the death of Josiah, after the death of the sponsor of the great reform which was based upon the scroll of Deuteronomy, a scroll which was understood to be God's word through Moses to the people, a scroll which really triggered a kind of "rediscovery" of Moses (we recall that the Passover was reestablished after a lapse of four hundred years)—the great question in Jeremiah's mind would be: Who will carry on the work of Moses if the scroll is now to be neglected? Is this the time for the prophet like Moses to appear?

From the task of being a prophet, he shrank. But Moses, too, hesitated in accepting his own call: the narrative in Exodus 4:1-17 is vivid with Moses' objections to God in the task which God was laying on him. Jeremiah, then, was like Moses *even in his hesitation.* Jeremiah felt boxed in. Moses' excuse to God was that he was an incompetent public speaker (Exodus 4:10); Jeremiah's, that he was too young (1:6). We have assumed him to be about eighteen years old.

We must pause now to say a word about the Israelite attitude toward the young. It was probably a good deal like the attitude of other peoples today in the Middle East toward their young people. Look at the traditional cultures of Turkey, of the Arab world, of Iran. Among these peoples it is the elders who have wisdom, who give orders and advice, who are looked up to. Young people defer to their elders and wait their turn until they are of suitable age themselves. Even the children sort themselves out by age: younger brothers defer to the eldest brother, who is always the boss. In our own culture there is a great deal of cultivation of youth and a great deal of envy on the part of older people for the vitality of young people. Think of the advertisements for carbonated drinks; we have never seen a pair of sixty-year-olds drinking some brand, with the caption "Look Older, Seem Wiser, Drink Our Cola!" But such was ever the case in Old Testament times, and Jeremiah felt the disability of his youth keenly. Who would ever listen to him?

There is some suspicion that the word "youth" here implies "bachelor." Jeremiah never married (16:1-2); he abstained from marriage as a public sign to the people that the end was near (16:3-9). Whether he felt that call to celibacy as a part of his perception of his *initial* call or not, it certainly became a part of his sensed call from God and may well have been there from the beginning. Here, then, is the spectacle of an eighteen-year-old youth, unmarried and never to be married, speaking out to his fellow citizens in the name of the Lord God Almighty and modeling his words after those of Moses of old.

The words which he would feel impelled to speak were not welcome to the people; we have indicated this already. And Jeremiah for his part could sense that there would be nothing but opposition ahead. This suspicion would be based not only on what he himself could calculate in the way of risks but more specifically, I think, on the worrisome words of Psalm 22, a psalm which was undoubtedly known to him.

Look at the first eleven verses of that psalm. Here is a picture of an Israelite who feels himself abandoned by God and hedged about with mocking foes. We are so accustomed to seeing this psalm as a description of Jesus, who spoke out the opening phrase of the psalm while hanging on the cross (Mark 15:34), that we forget for how many years that psalm had fed the souls of earlier Israelites. My suggestion here, however, is not that Jeremiah would have been alarmed in general by words that speak of abandonment by God, but specifically that this psalm would have seemed to Jeremiah a description of *Moses'* own experience. Look at verses 9-10 of the psalm. In Exodus 1:22 Pharaoh orders every

27

male child to be "cast" into the Nile; in Psalm 22:10 the poet says, "Upon thee was I cast from my birth" (and the Hebrew text uses the same verb). Indeed, the whole description of verses 9-10 fits the story of Moses' birth and infancy quite closely; Jeremiah surely would have heard these words as Moses' story and wondered whether accepting the task of being the prophet like Moses would not be a package deal, with persecution after the fashion of Psalm 22 as a part of the package.

Hence the necessity for Jeremiah, in 1:8, to hear reassurance from God that God would look after him. It may be good theology to say, as people do sometimes, that "one man with God is a majority," but it is still a frightening thing to be one man against a multitude; one had better be quite sure that God is with him, after all. What we have, then, is a kind of deal: If I, Jeremiah, am to speak for you, God, to your people, then you, God, are to look after me. This is the assumption upon which Jeremiah depends as he launches forth in his career, and it is this assumption which is at the root of the extraordinary complaints which he will lodge with God, complaints we shall examine at a later point (chapter VII).

The call is an awesome one; we have said that. But look at the wording of verse 10. It is a verse of tight-knit poetry; its structure can be seen better if we omit the middle two verbs ("to destroy and to overthrow"), which are the addition of a later editor. We then have:

> See, I have set you this day over nations and over kingdoms,
> to pluck up and to break down,
> to build and to plant.

The scope is international, and the task is both destructive and constructive. But destruction first, alas. Notice the nice X form of the four verbs of his task: to uproot and smash, build and plant: two verbs having to do with trees, and two verbs having to do with houses, arranged in an X form (what the analysts call "chiasmus," because the Greek letter chi is in the form of an X). And the verbs almost rhyme, too:

> *lintōsh welintōṣ*
> *libnōt welintōʿ.*

28

We shall become familiar with this kind of poetic skill on Jeremiah's part at many points in our study.

To the account of the call which we have been examining, there are appended two "visions," verses 11-14. We have no way of knowing whether these experiences came early in the prophet's career, but it is altogether likely that they did. The first concerns a sprig of flowering almond. Jeremiah was out walking one day and had a glimpse of the flowering almond; this reassured him that God would back up his word through Jeremiah to the people.

What is involved here? The almond blossom has the Hebrew name of "watcher" [shāqēd] presumably because in its early blooming it "watches" [shōqēd] for the spring. Some years ago a group of us from Beirut, Lebanon, were visiting the Jerusalem area. One morning during that visit our bus took us north of Jerusalem to the site of the biblical city of Gibeon. The spot is just a few miles west of Anathoth, as it happens. It was a foggy morning in February, and in the village where the ruins of the city are to be found, we glimpsed, through the white fog, a whole orchard of almond trees in full white blossom. It was a sight I shall never forget, and I have wondered since then whether it was not on such a morning as that one that Jeremiah caught his glimpse of the almond tree in bloom.

To Jeremiah the almond carried a message, and the message is wrapped up in the name of the blossom: as Jeremiah had seen the almond blossom (shāqēd), so God would be watching (shōqēd) over his word, to accomplish it. One can imagine Jeremiah's brooding over the whole issue of God's message to his people, and one can imagine, too, his wondering whether God meant business, to follow through on the word which the prophet felt impelled to speak. Does this word, too, have power? And brooding, brooding, over this one terrible question, Jeremiah found his attention caught by a glimpse of the almond. That glimpse came as an answer to his question, and the answer was in the form of a pun, a wordplay.

To us, a pun is usually a bad joke and little more; it is hard for us to imagine how word associations might be the bearers of serious thought, let alone of a message from God Almighty. But we must understand that different cultures have different understandings of these matters. In those days, evidently, the Israelites used word associations with the name of someone who

29

had died to create a dirge to mark his death. Nothing would seem more serious than a funeral lament. For example, the death of Abner (in Hebrew,'*abnēr*') suggested the word "fool" (in Hebrew, *nābāl*), so that David began his lament to Abner with the words, "Should Abner die as a fool dies (2 Sam. 3:33)?" Words, we have noticed, have power for the Israelites; and the power resides not only in their *meanings,* that give rise to action—words have power in their *sounds* as well, and words then become a channel for unexpected communication. To you and me, a word association does not seem like a very secure basis for faith in God, but it seemed secure enough to Jeremiah, and it is he whom we are trying to understand. And then again, there have been many other channels by which people through the centuries have claimed to receive word or strength from God—dreams, for example—that will seem undependable to the doubter and dependable to the believer.

A second vision of Jeremiah's is concerned not with the power behind the word from God but with the message, the content, of that word. Jeremiah sees a pot of water ready to boil, ready to spill over its water from the north. And its message seems equally clear to Jeremiah: disaster is boiling up out of the north for Judah. This terrible news will be spelled out in detail when Jeremiah speaks his oracles of the foe from the north (4:5 and thereafter).

The remainder of the chapter consists of various additions to these first intimations from God, but they do not alter the essential picture we have sketched.

We have come a long way in this chapter; we have tried to see the turmoil in the mind of the young Jeremiah in the context of the outer turmoil of the events at the beginning of Jehoiakim's reign. Jeremiah sensed the need of the moment for a prophet like Moses to continue the work of keeping God's word alive among the people. He sensed that he was to be that prophet, fight though he might against the task. And he accepted it, reluctantly, strengthened by the conviction that God would back up his word and back up his prophet who spoke the word.

And so the young man went out to preach. What he preached we must now consider.

Chapter III

God's People Turn Their Backs

Chapter 2 of the book of Jeremiah begins a collection of Jeremiah's "oracles," short utterances in poetic form from God to the people which he felt impelled to preach. The chapter opens with a short poem which stands by itself, a picture of the loyalty and faithfulness which Israel maintained to God in the early days of their relationship (verses 2-3):

> I remember the devotion of your youth,
>   your love as a bride,
> how you followed me in the wilderness,
>   in a land not sown.
> Israel was holy to the Lord,
>   the first fruits of his harvest.
> All who ate of it became guilty;
>   evil came upon them,
>   says the Lord.

Here, at the very beginning, we see many of the characteristics of Old Testament poetry and of Jeremiah's poetry in particular. We see the typical parallelism, in which a second line renews or reinforces the first line by a synonymous or supplementing image. We see the concentration of images and ideas, so that we are forced to listen to them slowly and explore their implications. Let us try it.

"Remember." Israelite remembering is not idle recollection. I might say, "I can't really remember what my grandfather looked like, he died so many years ago," and such a remark may be only of casual interest. But to the Israelite way of thinking, remembering is the way by which the past is recaptured in power for the present moment, almost as if there is a residue of energy in the past which can be appropriated and can make a real difference in the present situation. Thus for God to say that he remembers the devotion of Israel in the past suggests, so to speak, that he is taking the file marked "Israel" and moving it from the inactive to the active basket on his desk. God is going to *do* something about Israel's situation. "I am taking account of," "I am taking notice of," are clumsy paraphrases, but they will have to do. (Incidentally, this biblical view of memory has great consequence for the New Testament as well; when Jesus says, "Do this in remembrance of me," he is not urging us to hold a memorial service but rather to allow God to reenact the old event in all its present power.)

"Devotion." This important word (in Hebrew, *ḥesed*) is often translated "steadfast love" in the *Revised Standard Version* (for example, in the refrain of Psalm 136). It means the loyalty which two partners have for each other even when circumstances are no longer so happy. Husband and wife in a sturdy marriage stick by each other even when six kinds of disaster pile upon them at once. This is *ḥesed*. I am now taking account of the dogged fidelity you once showed to me in your honeymoon days—this is what is indicated here.

"In the wilderness" suggests "when disaster threatened"—no one is comfortable in a wilderness, where food and drink and security are at a minimum.

"Holy." This word had little of the stained-glass tone for Jeremiah that it has for us. Deep down, it had to do with those people or things or characteristics which belong to God, with what he owns or has charge of. "Israel belonged to God" is really what the phrase means here; Israel was special to him, Israel was set aside for his purposes. Nothing is said directly about her being morally pure—though that would be indirectly involved. Think of it this way: many churches keep a chalice on their altars, reserved for use in the service of communion. We would not think it appropriate to walk up to the altar on a hot day and use the chalice to have a drink of iced tea; it is simply not done. The

32

chalice is special, it belongs to communion. And Israel was special to God in just that way.

"The first fruits of his harvest." This phrase continues the image of "holy" as "belonging to God." Traditionally, whatever was first in the agricultural year belonged to God—the first lamb of the flock (Exodus 13:11-16), the first sheaf of wheat (Deuteronomy 26:1-4)—and there were ceremonies established for offering the first fruits to God (Deuteronomy 26:5-10). Here in 2:3, as later passages will indicate (2:21 and 5:10-11), Jeremiah evidently has the grape harvest in mind: Israel has been as special to God as the first fruits of the vintage are. (The prophet Isaiah, a hundred years earlier, offered the same idea: in Isaiah 5:1-7 the prophet sets forth a parable of Israel as the vineyard of God.)

Jeremiah continues the image in the next line: "All who ate of it became guilty"—any tribe or nation that tried to gain victory over Israel got into trouble for doing so. The verb translated here "became guilty" is hard to render rightly; it really means "took upon themselves the consequences of their wrongdoing." It is not just that those enemy peoples *found* themselves in the wrong; they *paid* for their wrongdoing as well, by suffering failure and defeat. Indeed, the balancing line says it: "evil" (or, better yet, "disaster") "came upon them." Militarily, socially, Israel was a success in those early days because she had remained utterly faithful to God. We might go on to say that Israel's wars against other nations in those days were holy wars, with God leading the army, strange though the idea may seem to us. So, at least, Jeremiah reads the past.

In passing, we may register our astonishment at this freedom which the prophets felt to explain the past in terms of their own present conception. Perhaps to some degree this is something we all do, but certainly the prophets did not feel any necessity to toe a party line in their interpretation of history. So there is a real contrast to this passage in Ezekiel 20:13. The prophet Ezekiel felt constrained to say that Israel had *never* been faithful to God, even in the wilderness period; Israel had always been rebellious. Perhaps each prophet found raw material in the nation's memories to serve as examples for his own reconstruction of the past.

Here, then, is Jeremiah's picture of the pristine purity of Israel: Israel had been faithful, and therefore successful, in the past.

33

This is in great contrast to the present situation, which he sets forth in a series of poems beginning with verse 5. These poems, by the way, are not necessarily placed in chronological order as we have them; instead, one senses here a kind of artistic order, the poem in verses 5-13 being placed directly after the poem of verses 2-3 to offer the strongest possible contrast.

> What wrong did your fathers find in me
>> that they went far from me,
> and went after worthlessness, and became worthless?
> They did not say, "Where is the Lord
>> who brought us up from the land of Egypt,
> who led us in the wilderness,
>> in a land of deserts and pits,
> in a land of drought and deep darkness,
>> in a land that none passes through,
>> where no man dwells?"
> And I brought you into a plentiful land
>> to enjoy its fruits and its good things.
> But when you came in you defiled my land,
>> and made my heritage an abomination.
> The priests did not say, "Where is the Lord?"
>> Those who handle the law did not know me;
>> the rulers transgressed against me;
>> the prophets prophesied by Baal,
>> and went after things that do not profit.
>
> Therefore I still contend with you,
>> says the Lord,
>> and with your children's children I will contend.
> For cross to the coasts of Cyprus and see,
>> or send to Kedar and examine with care;
>> see if there has been such a thing.
> Has a nation changed its gods,
>> even though they are no gods?
> But my people have changed their glory
>> for that which does not profit.
> Be appalled, O heavens, at this,
>> be shocked, be utterly desolate,
>>> says the Lord,

34

for my people have committed two evils:
    they have forsaken me,
the fountain of living waters,
    and hewed out cisterns for themselves,
broken cisterns,
    that can hold no water.

This poem does not need so much detailed comment as the earlier one did; we can follow the course of Jeremiah's argument quite easily. But there are a few details which we may note.

Look at verse 5:

What wrong did your fathers find in me
    that they went far from me,
and went after worthlessness, and became worthless?

The words "worthlessness" and "worthless" here represent the same Hebrew word (*hebel*) which begins the book of Ecclesiastes (translated there "vanity"). Evidently the word originally indicated "hot air" or "smoke"—that which is insubstantial, that which has no solidity. Jeremiah is using the term here to refer to pagan gods, but he is calling them "hot-air gods" not only to ridicule their undependability but also because the word he uses sounds a bit like "Baal," the designation for the fertility god to which many of the people were devoted.

There is a poignancy about the first two lines. On rereading it sounds almost like a hurt lover saying, "Sweetheart, what did I do wrong?" Many of us have grown up assuming that the God of the Old Testament is to be visualized as a deity with a white beard, sitting on a throne in heaven, smiting people here and there, and that it is only in the New Testament, from Jesus, that we learn of a God of love. One could question whether Jesus' words are always so reassuring (what do we do, for example, with the sayings recorded in Luke 6:24-26 or 17:2?), but one can definitely question any such assumption about the Old Testament in the light of a passage like this. Imagine: God the hurt lover! Now it is true that this question of God's in 2:5 is perhaps what we would call a rhetorical question—the situation is more that of a public trial in which God is indicting Israel for breach of contract (see especially verse 9 below)—but even for God to open

35

the legal argument with Israel by saying, "For the record, did I do anything wrong?" is to suggest the possibility of dialogue between God and the people in an extraordinary way. The Old Testament is constantly stretching us out beyond our conventional religious notions, and never more so than in the book of Jeremiah.

Perhaps it is worthwhile to note also that the verb "went," which we see twice in verse 5, is the same verb in Hebrew as "followed" in verse 2; this identity of wording is concealed by the English translation. Israel walked after God in the wilderness; since then Israel has walked after hot-air gods.

Let us pause here to examine this whole business of the Baal gods more closely. One of the most difficult aspects of Old Testament life for many of us to grasp is to understand what was so attractive about fertility worship. It is true, we may have our sex goddesses in the movies or use the hint of sexual cues in selling automobiles, but one is entertainment and the other is advertising, and we hardly see those aspects of our culture as worship in any sense of *ultimate* concern. How was it, we wonder, that thoughtful people could turn away from the worship of the God of Genesis and Exodus to gods and goddesses whose worship demanded cultic prostitution and drunkenness?

We must remind ourselves that this was an age without insurance policies, without social security, without savings accounts, without minted money even (that would be an invention in Lydia and Greece during the time Jeremiah was living, but minted coins would not be seen in Palestine for another hundred years). One's holdings were in land, in houses, in a few household possessions—but most of all in herds, flocks, and harvests. Herds, flocks, and harvests represented the margin between family prosperity and starvation, and a healthy number of sons and daughters represented one's margin of social security for old age (we can imagine the fearful infant mortality rate of those times). Hence much of one's security in the community was dependent upon the fertility of fields and livestock and upon one's own fertility too.

Palestine is largely unsuited to irrigation, that hedge against drought, and rainfall, though it usually comes, tends to be spotty. No wonder the Canaanites who lived on the land had developed fertility worship into a high art, and no wonder, too, that the

36

Israelites, as they themselves settled into agriculture, tended to adopt the Canaanite concerns and rituals. God, whom the Israelites called Yahweh, had been understood to be a God of holy war (verse 3 implied it, we noticed). But "baal" means nothing more than "lord" or "owner"—there was a baal for this field, another for that river, and still another for the spring yonder—so Baal was a kind of all-purpose term, and there must have been a good deal of blending of the worship of Yahweh and of Baal (Who knows? they must have thought; perhaps Baal is simply another name for Yahweh after all!). So it was that King Saul could name one of his sons Eshbaal, meaning something like "man of Baal" (1 Chronicles 8:33; the form in 2 Samuel 2:8, Ish-bosheth, is a censored version of the name). We are not to assume that King Saul worshiped Baal rather than Yahweh, but simply that he casually identified the two. This seems to be the burden of Elijah's challenge to Israel a hundred and fifty years after Saul (1 Kings 18:21): the two deities are different; you must choose. But so frantic was the search for fertility that it must have been very difficult to give up these practices. No Baal image, so far as I know, has as yet been unearthed in Palestine from any Israelite period, but dozens of little figurines of Astarte, the fertility goddess, have been dug up; women must have been particularly prone to indulge in such worship (compare Jeremiah 44:15).

High in the Lebanese mountains is a lovely site called Afqa. Near there the river Ibrahim emerges out of a cavern in the mountains and makes its way down through steep valleys until it flows out into the Mediterranean Sea, just south of the old Phoenician port of Byblos. It is clear from both archaeological evidence and from ancient authors that Byblos was a center for fertility worship, and so, too, was that site high in the mountains where the river came out of the cavern; its greater flow in the spring was the sign to the worshiper that Baal had renewed his lease on life for the coming year. It is an extraordinary place, spooky inside the cavern, truly a fit place for the worship of the forces of nature. Now, across from the entrance to the cavern one may see the foundations of an ancient temple to Astarte, the fertility goddess—it must have been an imposing structure in its time—and by one corner of the foundations there remains the stump of an old tree, from which still new-sprouting twigs grow. To these twigs are tied white strips of cloth torn from the gar-

37

ments of ill or barren women in the villages of the region—both Orthodox Christian and Muslim women resort to the practice. Next to the stump is a little shrine, with a crude painting of the Virgin Mary inside; the first time I visited the spot and looked into the shrine, a candle was burning. Now think: for at least fifteen hundred years the temple has been in ruins, and it is the Virgin Mary rather than Astarte that has been venerated; yet the prayers offered up at the spot are plainly still the same. Such is the everlasting, understandable hunger for health and children, and such must have been the passion of the Israelites in the days when Jeremiah preached.

Well, we might wonder, this is åll very natural; what is so harmful about it? In days before medical science, in days before public and private agencies organized help for the helpless of society, what was so harmful about fertility worship?

The problem, as the prophets saw it, was not necessarily in the excesses of sexuality and drunkenness in the cultic celebrations, which might well alarm us, though this was certainly an aspect of the problem. The problem was that the Baals, in people's mind, tended to be cosmic bellhops, so to speak, ready to grant goodies to the people if only the people offered them adequate tips; whereas Yahweh, the God of the covenant, would grant the blessings of fertility to a people who remained sensitive to the expectations of ethical behavior in the covenant. (For further portrayals of the struggle between the worship of the Baals and the worship of Yahweh, see Hosea 2:4-8—"their mother" in verse 4 is a figure for Israel, "lovers" in verse 5 represents the Baal gods, and "my first husband" of course is Yahweh—or look at Deuteronomy 28:1-6.) Yahweh deals with his people not on the basis of tit for tat but on the basis of grace and mercy, in response to the sensitivity which the people manifest to Yahweh's will. In short, what was at stake between the worship of the Baals and the worship of Yahweh was the quality of the relationship between the people and the deity. People tended to think of the Baals as transactional gods whose main job was giving goodies and to forget questions of the quality of life altogether.

All this is implied by the warm, sad words of God in Jeremiah 2:5.

Verse 6 characterizes Yahweh more closely; he is the God of the exodus out of Egypt. It is curious: we tend to feel that the

38

specificity of such a "creed" is limiting. We want our creeds to be general, and so we talk first about God in creation. "I believe in God the Father Almighty, maker of heaven and earth," we begin. But Israel never began with the generality of creation but always with the specificity of the act of rescue out of Egypt. Think of the beginning of the Ten Commandments: "I am the Lord your God, who brought you out of the land of Egypt, out of the house of bondage (Exod. 20:2)." Always Israel began there. It is as if the Old Testament people sensed that creation is not a secure way to begin to characterize God, since creation has within it not only the glories of sunset and stars, the marvels of life together in families, but the terrors of earthquake and the fearful death of plague as well. But if we begin our story with the rescue from Egypt, we know right away that God is a God of grace and mercy, a God who is *better* than we expect. Look at the way the nightmarish descriptions of the desert pile up in this verse; who would want to linger in a land where the darkness is appalling, in a land that no one lives in? (You and I, in our crowded world, crave solitude often; not so the Israelites, who craved company and the security of the village and town above all!) And God led us even through the wilderness. As an analogy one can imagine an eleven-year-old boy reminding his younger brother how last month he got him home past the graveyard by the dark of the moon at eleven o'clock when the owls went *hoo!*—and he'd better not forget it, either.

Verse 7 brings a contrast: the lovely land, the plentiful land, literally a land of orchards, a land which then the people, according to the accusation, polluted and made unclean. And the leadership is very much to blame—priests and prophets (verse 8).

The general situation is clear: Israel has turned her back on Yahweh and his gracious acts and has gone off instead after fertility gods. So now God sums up his indictment. For it is an indictment here, as the legal language of verse 9 makes clear; "contend" in Hebrew really means "call to law, sue, indict." Since it is the fathers who went astray (verse 5), God will continue the indictment even with the grandchildren (verse 9). For go as far west or as far east as you please (verse 10), has there ever been a precedent for a nation's switching gods? Why, the pagan nations are more loyal to their nonexistent gods than Israel is to the true God. What irony this is! And now the summary to the

39

witnesses (the heavens, verse 12, function in this cosmic law-court scene as a kind of jury): my people have abandoned me (verse 13), the spring which always gives forth running water, and have resorted instead to cisterns dug out of the soft limestone and prepared to catch the rainwater. Now a cistern that stores water is by no means the equivalent of a spring which produces water on its own, but even so, it may suffice—unless it leaks, as these cisterns do. Here is a perfect summary image of the uselessness of the Baal gods. We should remind ourselves here how precious water is in a dry and thirsty land (compare Psalm 63:1). To be out on a summer hike and to have planned for one's noon destination a spot where there has been water in the past, only to find there no water at all by which to slake one's thirst—that is a terrible thing. One can go without food for many days, but not water. And in a land where water cannot always be depended on, Jeremiah's contrast between the dependable spring and the useless cisterns makes a telling climax.

Further poems in the chapter (verses 14-19, 20-25, 26-37) continue the theme of God's disappointment in Israel's unfaithfulness, and it is not hard to follow their imagery. A few remarks will suffice here. In contrast to the honeymoon days of Israel, when other nations that attacked Israel were defeated (verse 3), now the foreign nations feel free to attack, just as a lion roars confidently over his prey (verses 14-15). Egypt in particular has humiliated Judah (Memphis and Tahpanhes in verse 16 are Egyptian cities). And (to carry on the water image of verse 13), since the broken cisterns have not satisfied Judah's thirst, she has gone off either to Egypt or to Assyria, alternately, to "drink the water"—that is, to seek foreign aid (verse 18).

Verses 20-25 explore in greater detail the image of harlotry. We must understand that what is meant here is not only the actual prostitution of the fertility ceremonies but more particularly the figurative prostitution of Israel's adherence to the Baal gods rather than to her true Lord, Yahweh. "Bowed down" in verse 20 is perhaps a misleading translation; the Hebrew is much uglier— "sprawled" would be better (compare *The New English Bible:* "you sprawled in promiscuous vice"). The vine image in verse 21 picks up the "first fruits" image of verse 2, reflecting the picture of Israel as the vineyard of God which was earlier set forth in Isaiah 5:1-7. And the stain image of verse 22 picks up another

40

utterance of Isaiah's, found in Isaiah 1;15-17. Each prophet assumed that his hearers already had their ears full of the earlier pronouncements of earlier prophets; it is hard for us always to catch the previous references in the later variations before us. This is why it is true that the more one reads elsewhere in biblical material, the more one understands what one is reading at a given point.

Let us look for a moment at the animal imagery in verses 23-24, because it provides a good example of how misunderstandings can creep into the commentaries. Scholars have assumed that both the camel and the wild ass described here are female animals in heat, and several German commentators and at least one important American commentator have cut out the reference to the wild ass as a presumably unauthentic addition to the text which overloads the poetry and spoils the original sequence of ideas which Jeremiah intended; *The Jerusalem Bible* and *The New English Bible* have followed this assumption.[1] But some years ago a colleague who had lived and worked for many years in rural Egypt told me that the commentators simply do not understand how these animals actually behave. It seems, he said, that the female camel does not experience sexual heat; she is quite casual when the male seeks her out. The point of the camel image here is that the camel is young, and young camels cannot walk straight; when a young camel gets loose in the marketplace, everyone scrambles out of the way, because no one knows where the camel will step next. "A restive young camel, interlacing her tracks." The female wild ass, however, is another story. When her season comes, she is frantic for the male and seeks to track him down by the scent of the urine which he has deposited. When she picks up the scent, she goes frantic with joy and races off to find the male. "A wild ass . . . in her heat sniffing the wind! Who can restrain her lust?" The point is, the young camel cannot walk straight, and the female wild ass in heat cannot be diverted from racing straight to her sexual goal; neither of these animals is particularly "responsible," and both of them are equally striking images of Judah gone astray. The lines about the wild ass, then, are not an addition to the text; they belong here.

In verse 27 Jeremiah seems to have switched the sex references ironically—a leafy tree, after all, is a suitable symbol of female fertility, and a standing stone of male fertility, rather than as

Jeremiah gives them. That he should identify the sex references wrongly is part of his sarcasm. [2]

And a remark about verse 28: the ancient Greek translation has preserved two extra lines to the verse that have unaccountably dropped out of the traditional Hebrew text. The last part of the verse should evidently read:

> For as many as your cities
> are your gods, O Judah,
> and as many as your streets, O Jerusalem,
> are your altars to Baal.

The closing verses in the chapter pick up many of the images with which we have become familiar earlier; there is, it seems, nothing ahead for Judah but humiliation (verses 36-37).

Chapter 3 begins a fresh series of poems on the theme of Judah's disloyalty. The chapter is interrupted by two sections of prose which appear to have been added to the poetic material at a later stage in the building up of the book of Jeremiah, but the four poems which belong here are evidently verses 1-5, 12b-14a (that is, the last half of verse 12 through the first half of verse 14), 19-20, and 21-25. Though these poems, as I have indicated, continue the theme of harlotry, there is a new note: these poems are united by the Hebrew verb translated "turn" or "return," a word which Jeremiah exploits in a wide range of meanings.

Verse 1 deals with a common domestic legal situation, but Jeremiah's second question—"Would not that land be greatly polluted?"—leaves us saying, "How's that again?" The logic escapes us. And it evidently escaped the ancient Greek translator as well, because the Greek text gives the question as "Would not that *woman* be greatly polluted?" But Jeremiah evidently meant "land," after all, and was thinking of Deuteronomy 24:4, whereby the land incurs guilt when a former husband takes a wife who has belonged to another back again. [3] The point of the verse here, then, is: Judah has done something irrevocable; God could hardly be expected to take her back even if he wanted to. The rest of the poem of verses 1-5 is quite clear, although two things might be noted. First, the Hebrew verb translated "lain with" in verse 2 was evidently considered in such poor taste in ancient times that a

42

less offensive verb has always been substituted for it in the public reading of the Hebrew scriptures; even "ravished" (*The New English Bible*) is not as strong as the Hebrew word evidently was. And then the reference to "an Arab in the wilderness" sounds offensive today; one is impelled, on first reading, to assume that Jeremiah was making a disparaging remark about the lustfulness of Arabs, but it is evidently not so; he had in mind, rather, the image of Bedouins, who lived by raiding, waiting to waylay a caravan.[4]

Verse 3 suggests that drought has come upon the land because of the people's disloyalty to God. This theme is to be found everywhere in the preaching of the prophets; we have mentioned Elijah's announcement of the drought (1 Kings 17:1), and the prophet Amos offers a particularly vivid example of this idea (see Amos 4:7-8). Now to Christians of an earlier age, such an idea caused no trouble, but to those of us who watch the weather reporter on the evening television news explaining to us where the high and low pressure areas are, it becomes difficult to accept without difficulty the idea that rainfall patterns are primarily an index of the current state of morality of the nation in question. What are we to say? Much could be said, but this at least: that the prophets saw the quality of life in Israel as the central question, and everything that pertained to that life, in the affairs of international relations or in the natural world, revolved around that quality of life in Israel. We shall have occasion to look into this matter further in the next chapter.

The image of Israel as the "wife" of Yahweh is intermixed in this chapter with the image of Israel as the "children" of Yahweh. Israel calls God "my father" in verse 4, and similarly in verse 19, but in verse 20, as in verse 1, the relationship is assumed to be that of husband and wife. Both these images go back to the prophet Hosea a hundred years before: Hosea 1—3 sets forth the image of Israel as wife to Yahweh, but in Hosea 11 the image is that of sonship. The prophet Ezekiel will solve the tension later by his allegory (Ezekiel 16) of Israel as the foundling baby girl, exposed to die but adopted by Yahweh as his daughter and then espoused to him as bride when she came of age. For the moment we can only say that the inconsistency is real in the material of Jeremiah, but it did not seem worrisome to Jeremiah himself. It

43

may be, for example, that "my father" (verse 4) was a common address of wife to husband (some Arabic dialects are reported to have such an idiom), but the plurality of Israel's population encourages the plural address "O children" or "O sons" of verses 14 and 22. The point is simple—the basic question is this: To whom does Israel belong? Wives belong to husbands, and children belong to parents. The specific relationship is of secondary importance, but the identification of who it is to whom Israel belongs is all important.

One more detail from this chapter, and we must round off this survey of chapters 2 and 3. In verse 14 we find the phrase "for I am your master," and in verse 24 the phrase "the shameful thing has devoured." Both these phrases mask references to Baal. In the phrase in verse 14, Jeremiah has used a verb derived from the noun "baal"—"I have 'lorded' you," meaning something like "I have been your (real) 'Baal.'" Remember, the word "baal" simply means "lord, owner." "One master is *not* like another; you have one true master, and the rest are false. So do not seek after the Baal gods; the title 'Baal' really belongs to me, to Yahweh." And in the second phrase, in verse 24, the Hebrew word *bosheth*, which really means "shame," was the standard euphemism for "Baal." Earlier we took note of the fact that one of Saul's sons was named Eshbaal (1 Chronicles 8:33), but the form recorded in 2 Samuel 2:8, we noticed, was Ishbosheth, which I called a censored version of the name, and the euphemism "bosheth" is substituted for "baal" in the name. Jeremiah uses the euphemism here in 3:24 because he is anticipating the phrase "let us lie down in our *shame*" in verse 25. In every way he can, then, Jeremiah is ringing the changes on the whole matter of the false relationship between Israel and the Baal gods, and the true relationship between Israel and Yahweh which the nation has rejected.

Chapter 2 began with the poignant question of the hurt lover, "What wrong did your fathers find in me?" (2:5). Chapter 3 voices God's appeal for the kind of genuine repentance which he would like to see Israel manifest: "Return, faithless Israel.... Only acknowledge your guilt" (verses 12, 13); "Return, O faithless sons, I will heal your faithlessness" (verse 22). I mentioned earlier that this chapter works on the various meanings of "return" or "turn." But no English translation can

44

communicate by any wordplay the piling up of words related to "turn" in these passages; in that last phrase, the Hebrew sounds something like "Return, turnable sons, and I will heal your turnings." How strange that Israel should find it so easy to turn away from God and so hard to turn back!

We cannot linger over the meaning of the prose insertions (verses 6-11 and 15-18); the interested reader may consult a recent commentary.[5] But one basic question should perhaps be discussed: Does the imagery of these poems, heavy with sexuality as it is, really communicate to a modern reader, or does such imagery perhaps prove too offensive to seem to speak of the things of faith? Many folk go to the Bible for a higher vision than the world affords, for lofty vistas which draw them out of the shabbiness of day-to-day living. To such folk the blunt language of Jeremiah may seem unattractive at best, a stumbling block at worst. What can we say to this?

Much, but this at least: the biblical faith never claims to take people out from the world but testifies, in fact, to a God who enters our world, loves it, gives his Son for it. The biblical faith does not emphasize a "spiritual" part of humankind at all but sees us whole, our cravings and hungers and lusts as well as our ideals and hopes and dreams. The Bible speaks of our "knowing" God, and of God's "knowing" us, but "knowing," in the Old Testament, is not factual acquaintance with but rather intimate relationship with; notice the striking use of "know" in Genesis 4:1 to refer to sexual relations. If biblical knowledge is typified by the relation of the marriage bed, then marriage-gone-wrong is a vivid picture to put in contrast to marriage-which-should-go-right. Hosea's language seems like that of a rural person who minces no words (Hosea 2:2-5); Jeremiah uses some of the same sexual imagery, but with far greater warmth and lyricism. This is why we have been speaking of God as the hurt lover.

Perhaps it is best said in the phrasing of 2:27: "For they have turned their back to me, and not their face." The Hebrew word "back" here means "the back of the neck." In Exodus 32:9 the people are called "stiff-necked," and it is the same word: the back of their neck is stiff; they are stubborn. So here in Jeremiah, the prophet perceives God to be saying, The people have turned the back of the neck to me rather than their face. How can God carry on a conversation with the back of a neck? How can he

45

bring his people to the point of turning around once more, saying "I'm sorry," and reembarking on the great relationship with him? What kind of God is this who is desolate that his great project has gone astray, who is baffled by such stubbornness? What can he do? What will he do?

Jeremiah's sense of what God is about to do we shall explore in the next chapter.

Chapter IV

God Declares War on His People

With 4:5 we are in a new situation. Up to now the poetry has been heavy with the language of sexuality, with love gone wrong; now we are in the context of war. (Curious, is it not, how these two "fulfilling" experiences are so often linked in our folk wisdom? "All's fair in love and war," we say, or "Make love, not war.") The imagery is now of battles and panic, of soldiers and sieges and lamentation—the wording of verses 5-8 of chapter 4 is typical of what we shall find for several chapters.

There is something else that is new here too: not only do we have a new set of images, we have dialogue. When we look back to chapters 2-3, we find that almost all the oracles there must be understood as words of God to the people; there were no words of God to Jeremiah or Jeremiah to God, no words of Jeremiah to the people or of the people to Jeremiah. We had a dialogue between God and Jeremiah—understandably, in chapter 1, in Jeremiah's call—and these other kinds of address we shall see in the course of the book of Jeremiah, but chapters 2 and 3 contain almost solely the words of God to the people. The only exception (beyond the prose commentary of 3:6-11, which is unoriginal) is the "repentance" of 3:22b-25, and really we cannot be sure whether this is a quotation by Jeremiah of what people are actually saying to God or whether it is Jeremiah's understanding of what God *wishes* the people would say to him. In any event, the passage does not take up a major share of chapters 2-3.

In 4:5 and beyond, however, we hear a variety of speakers, and

47

the speakers are addressing various audiences. Thus in 4:5 and following, God speaks, while in 4:19 and following, Jeremiah speaks, evidently to himself. The more one looks at the material here, the more insistent becomes the question: In a given instance, who is speaking and who is being addressed? Sometimes the context makes it clear; thus 4:6 *has* to be spoken by God ("I bring evil from the north"). But sometimes it is not at all clear, and one must resort to parallel and balancing passages elsewhere to begin to tease out of the material the identification of speakers. I shall not burden the reader here with the argumentation that leads to the identifications I have made, but I shall indicate my identification of speakers as we proceed; because identifying the speaker is part of what we need to understand the passages fully.

Let us look, then, at 4:5-8. Verses 5-7 are spoken by God, but verse 8 is spoken by Jeremiah to the people, and the last line is his quotation of what the people's wailing is to be (the conjunction "for" before the phrase "the fierce anger" is in error). We should therefore render verse 8 as follows:

Jeremiah: For this gird you with sackcloth,
            lament and wail:
         "The fierce anger of the Lord
          has not turned back from us."

The subquotation, then, is the content of the people's wailing which Jeremiah is urging upon the people.

Now what is God saying to the people? The exact functional equivalent today of the first line of his announcement in verse 5 would be "Sound the air-raid sirens through the land." The contrast between a city and a village in those days was not size, though that inevitably entered into the picture; the contrast was defense walls—a city had them, while the surrounding villages did not. The consequence, then, was that at the approach of any invading army, the signals would be given, and the farmers and tradesmen would drop their work on the spot, gather up their wives and children and servants, and make for the city, hoping that they could all get there before the city gates were closed and barred and hoping, too, that the city fathers had made adequate provision for food and water within the city for a siege. (Compare the similar images of impending disaster, and its impact on the

48

villagers, in Mark 13:14 18.) Sieges in ancient times could last a long time; Nebuchadnezzar besieged the Phoenician city of Tyre for thirteen years before it surrendered! And Jerusalem itself in its final besieging by Nebuchadnezzar would hold out for a year and a half (approximately January 588 to July 587 B.C.).

The term "lion" in verse 7 is an old image for the invader from Mesopotamia; we saw it in 2:15, and Isaiah had used it a hundred years before (Isaiah 5:26-30). The result of the invasion will be that the land will become a waste and the cities uninhabitable; this is ominous, if the signal has been sounded through the land, and the cities have been resorted to as refuges for the population (verse 5). The identity of the enemy, then, as I have already suggested in chapter II, is Babylonia. One might object that Babylonia is not north of Jerusalem at all, but east. On a map of the whole Middle East this is true, but Jeremiah was considering the matter from a local perspective. An invader marching west from Babylon to Palestine would actually follow the Euphrates River north as well as west and then cut across to the city of Aleppo; then march straight south through Hama (the biblical Hamath) to Damascus; then farther south, crossing the Jordan River at Hazor; then south to Jerusalem or else south along the coast of Palestine and east to Jerusalem. But the main thrust of such an invader would be south from Aleppo and Damascus, and this is what Jeremiah had in mind.

He seems to have had something else in mind, too. There were old mythic ideas floating around in the subconscious minds of the Israelites, ideas of the gathering of pagan gods in the far north to plot disaster for people. That gathering place of the gods in the far north is referred to more than once in the Old Testament: the mythical nation of Gog comes from the uttermost parts of the north (Ezekiel 38:15), God's own splendor comes out of the north (Job 37:22), and Psalm 48:2-3 most curiously identifies that gathering place in the north with Zion in Jerusalem, the mountain of Yahweh. The "north" therefore represented a kind of never-never land to Jeremiah's hearers, and the announcement in 4:6 would be received with a special kind of horror.

The basic point of verses 5-7 is not, however, the details of military preparation for siege or the identity of the besieger; it is that God himself has taken action against his people, God has initiated the process by which the invader is coming. Not even that God has *allowed* the invader to slip in; no, God *intends* the invader to come and lay waste the land. Recall, now, that the whole understanding of Israel's covenant was that Yahweh would defend Israel against her enemies and defeat them (2:3)—more, even: that Yahweh would lead Israel in holy war (compare Exodus 15:3: "The Lord is a man of war"). Now, suddenly, because Israel has broken the covenant with God, God has declared holy war *against* Israel. Israel is now the enemy of God. One has the feeling that one might be able to handle a human enemy; but to be opposed by God who brings on, who sponsors, an enemy is to be in a one-sided fight indeed. No wonder Jeremiah urges the people to lamentation and wailing, urges them to cry, "The fierce anger of the Lord has not turned back from us."

The little poem in verses 5-8 begins with a description of the battle. Similar descriptions are found in verses 13-18 and verses 29-31. Both these poems vary the speaker as the poem of verses 5-8 did. The poem of verses 29-31 has a similar pattern to that of verses 5-8: God speaks first (verses 29-30), then Jeremiah speaks (verse 31), and the verse ends with a quotation of the people. The pattern of speakers in verses 13-18 is more complicated, however: God speaks in verse 13, but the last line is an interruption by the people. Then Jeremiah speaks in verse 14, God speaks in verses 15-17, and Jeremiah rounds off the passage by speaking in verse 18. These three poems are separated from each other by two interludes (verses 9-12 and 19-28). It begins to look as if the material in verses 5-31 is very carefully structured. Let us look more closely at the content of this material.

The word translated "courage" in verse 9 is literally "heart," but for the Israelites the heart is the seat not of the emotions so much as of planning, of decision-making: the civil leaders, then, will become paralyzed by this turn of events, and the religious leaders likewise. In verse 10 Jeremiah complains to God that God has "deceived" the people; the verb is the same as that found in Genesis 3:13, where the serpent "beguiled" the woman so that she ate from the fruit. By what means would God do this? No doubt through fair-weather prophets who continued to speak a happy and encouraging word in dark times; 6:13-14 depicts a similar picture, and we have the narrative in chapter 28 of Jeremiah's encounter with such a fair-weather prophet,

50

Hananiah—we shall study the narrative in more detail in chapter VI. But why would God want to do such a thing? Why, oh why, would God want to deceive, to beguile his people? There are several kinds of answers to this question. One is that at this stage of Israel's history it was understood that God was capable of leading his people astray when he wanted to. A really funny incident along this line is narrated in 1 Kings 22:1-38, when the prophet Micaiah explains why the fair-weather prophets of the king were enabled (falsely) to foretell success while he, Micaiah, foretold failure: the prophets spoke for God all right, said Micaiah, but they spoke deceptively. But on another level one can still ask, "But given this frame of mind, why, still, in Jeremiah's mind, would God want to mislead his people at this zero hour?" And to this question one might answer, not altogether flippantly, "That's what Jeremiah would like to know." He is baffled by the circumstance that so many priests and prophets who claim to speak for God, and whose credentials Jeremiah cannot easily challenge, should be reassuring the people at this point of history. The word "life," here, really means "inner self," perhaps "breath, throat": the sword is held to the people's throat—why should they speak easy words?

A new image comes in verses 11-12: of a hot wind. The normal, prevailing wind in Palestine comes out of the northwest, from the sea, bringing moisture. The breeze comes up particularly in the cool of the day (compare Genesis 3:8), and then the farmer uses the breeze to winnow his grain; the breeze blows the light chaff aside while the heavier grain falls at his feet. But occasionally the wind shifts and comes in from the desert, from the east, heavy with heat and dryness. The humidity plunges. The geographer Denis Baly recalls once, when the desert wind was blowing across Haifa, feeling the shaving cream dry on his face before he could put razor to it.[1] Such is God's judgment when it comes.

With verse 13 God once more speaks in fresh images of the battle to come, and the people respond once more in lament. Jeremiah interjects an appeal to repentance; it was traditionally one of the tasks of the prophet to interpret God's will to the people and then to appeal to the people for a change of heart (for a similar appeal, see Isaiah 1:16-17, 19-20). And once again God describes what is coming (verses 15-17), and Jeremiah (verse 18) offers interpretation.

51

The second interlude begins with Jeremiah's frantic meditation, his description of his own physical response to the battle which he has perceived with his inner ear and eye. The words translated "my anguish, my anguish" are in Hebrew literally "my bowels, my bowels" (so the *King James Version*), for the bowels were understood to be the seat of violent emotion (compare, for example, Job 30:27, where the *King James Version* reads "my bowels boiled, and rested not"). All of us understand how we feel when an emergency suddenly hits us, and the adrenaline pumps into our bloodstream, and our heart thumps, and we feel fear at the pit of our stomach. Jeremiah describes his reaction in this fashion. In verse 20 the words "disaster follows hard on disaster" are literally "people cry out, 'collapse on collapse,' "—one imagines people's roof beams collapsing as they burn, pottery storage jars shattering beneath, and the shouts of people in confusion. "Tents" and "curtains" are to be taken here in a figurative sense; the overtone of these words may be almost precisely what English-speaking people mean by "homes," not the house buildings only, but all the warmth of life within. And by verse 21 Jeremiah is asking himself how long he must envision the signal flag and suffer the trumpet to sound in his inner ear—images with which we began in verses 5-6.

And suddenly God interrupts, cool as can be (verse 22); he speaks like a quiet schoolmaster, explaining what is going on. The people are stupid, they have not been learning their lessons properly. There is a nice little wordplay here, I think: Jeremiah has begun with "my bowels" (in Hebrew, *me'ay*), but God's first word reverses the first two consonants (the reverse apostrophe is a throat consonant): "my people" (in Hebrew, *'ammī*). It is as if God were saying, Jeremiah, you may be agitated about your bowels, but I am more concerned about my people.

The poem in verses 23-26, in which Jeremiah once more speaks, is one of the most appalling in the Bible, and at the same time one of the most beautiful. It is very carefully put together, like a delicate piece of jewelry. Four times the verses begin with "I looked." Looked at what? At four visions of non-life (earth, heavens, mountains, hills), and at four visions of life (man, birds, fruitful land, cities). They are nicely balanced: man lives on earth, birds in the heavens. The images of verse 23 carry us back to Genesis 1: "waste and void" is the same Hebrew phrase as "without form and void" in Genesis 1:2, and of course "no light" is the negation of Genesis 1:3. At the same time the image of verse 25 carries us back to Genesis 2:5 ("and there was no man to till the ground"). The imagery of verse 26 is that of the Israelites entering into Palestine: "fruitful land" is the same Hebrew word as "plentiful land" in Jeremiah 2:7, and "desert" of course was mentioned in 2:6. We move, in other words, from the concern with creation in verses 23 and 25 to the concern with the covenant people and Palestine in verse 26.

Now on first glance the order of images in this poem strikes us as anticlimactic, like that curious slogan current at the university in New Haven, Connecticut, "For God, for country, and for Yale"; we might feel a bit more comfortable if the order of terms were reversed! But we must recall what we learned when we were discussing 2:6 (in chapter III)—that in the Old Testament one begins with redemption, with the liberation of the exodus. Here in this passage we find that redemption is the climax, the ultimate purpose of God's efforts. The ultimate concern of God is the quality of life of the community. If that is gone, if the rescued people have forgotten their rescuer, then all of creation may as well go down the drain as well. Jeremiah envisages a time of chaos and dark night, when confusion reigns as it reigned before God's spirit began to brood over the face of the waters (Genesis 1:2). Thus Jeremiah's vision, and God's antiphonal reinforcement of the vision (verse 28) does nothing to lighten the gloom (verse 27 may be a later addition to the text; or again it may be that in verse 27 only the word "not" is an addition, and the rest of the verse is the first part of God's reponse, in which case "yet" should be translated "and").

Verse 29 brings us back into the field of battle once more. It is possible that the first line should be translated, "At the shout, 'Horseman and archer!' every city takes to flight," so that we would have here one more battle cry. The phrase "O desolate one" in verse 30 is ungrammatical in Hebrew and missing in the text of one of the ancient versions; it should be omitted here. God is contemptuously addressing the land as a prostitute attracting customers; Jeremiah's counter-image (verse 31) is of a woman gasping as if in childbirth, moaning "Woe is me," as the people said "woe to us" in verse 13.

Here, then (verses 5-31), is the first section of material on the

53

foe from the north. There are six more sections, all shorter than the first: 5:1-9, 5:10-17, 5:20-29, 6:1-8, 6:9-15, 6:16-30. Now that we have worked through the first section with some care, the reader can read these subsequent sections without too much further guidance. Let us note a few points, however.

It slowly becomes apparent that the coming battle which God has planned is intended as a teaching device (compare 4:22). Thus God asks for an honest man (5:1), but the people have no sense (5:4); God therefore must punish them (5:9).

The destruction or pruning of the vines (5:10) is metaphorical, for the vine is Israel, a people who are intended to belong to the Lord (2:3) but who do not, as a matter of fact (5:10). One then gets (5:14) a picture of the destructiveness of the prophetic word (we have already noted this image in chapter II), followed by a terrifying description of the foe in 5:15-17 (what a contrast with 2:3!); in the honeymoon days all who ate of Israel were punished, whereas now they will simply eat and eat and eat (5:17). Can you imagine how villagers feel when an occupying army comes into their village whose language they do not understand (5:15)? Today an Arab resident of east Jerusalem may be terrified by a notice in his mailbox written in Hebrew; he cannot read it, what does it say? It may be nothing more than a telephone bill, but a message from the occupying power written in a language one cannot read may bring on panic.

The section 5:20-29 is the central one of the seven on the foe from the north and offers God's lesson to his refractory pupils. Even the chaotic sea stays within bounds as it should (5:22), but the people by contrast are persistently out of bounds (verses 23-24).

The section 6:1-8 offers battle scenes once more, including (for the first time) a couple of shouts from the besieging enemy themselves (6:4-5). The next section once more offers a metaphorical order to deal with the vineyard Israel, and finally, once more, God's concern that the people have not learned their lesson (6:16-21). It looks, actually, as if we have a conversation between God and Jeremiah here; in verse 16, God speaks, but the end of the verse ("But they said...") is spoken by Jeremiah; and again in verse 17 God speaks, but the last line ("But they said...") is spoken by Jeremiah. God then continues the announcement (verses 18-21) of what is to happen.

54

Verses 22-26 form a kind of recapitulation, a complicated dialogue which precisely balances the pattern of the complicated one in 4:13-18. Here in chapter 6 we find the description of the foe by God (verses 22-23), then the people's statement of their paralysis and pain (verse 24), then God's warning (verse 25), then finally Jeremiah's appeal to the people to gird on sackcloth (just like 4:8), ending again with a quotation of the people's lamentation (and again, as in 4:8, the conjunction "for" is erroneous):

Jeremiah: O daughter of my people, gird on sackcloth,
                  and roll in ashes;
             make mourning as for an only son,
                  most bitter lamentation:
             " How suddenly the destroyer
                  will come upon us."

Finally in verses 27-30 we have a kind of postscript; really, it is God's final examination of the people, again in the schoolroom image. He deputizes Jeremiah to do the examining (verse 27), and Jeremiah brings back the report (verses 28-30) that they have failed the examination. It is hopeless. It really is hopeless.

We see, then, a cycle of seven sections that deal with the climactic war to come, giving it a meaning; it is a teaching device by God the schoolmaster. These seven sections are set within a kind of prelude (4:1-4) and postlude (8:4-10a and 13).[2] This prelude and postlude balance each other, we notice, in that both of them contain a similar turn of phrase involving "turning" or "returning" (4:1a and 8:4b), and this framing structure of prelude and postlude, with the verb "(re)turn," is thus tied closely to chapter 3, where that same verb turns up frequently. We shall have more to say about the structure of this material in chapter V.

Curiously enough, to these seven sections dealing with the foe from the north were added three more later on: 8:14—9:9, 9:17-22, and 10:17-25. These sections appear by no means to be a kind of afterthought, but on the contrary they deepen and darken the picture of the doom ahead. Let us now take account of these.

The material of 8:14 begins by mimicking 4:5, but with a new twist: the people do say, "Let us assemble and go into the fortified cities," as they were bidden to do in 4:5, but then they add, "and perish there"! God again offers images of battle (as in 4:13, 15), and Jeremiah again gives voice to his own reaction to the emergency (8:18-21, like 4:19-21). We have a remarkable interchange in 8:19: the people are wondering, business-as-usual, whether God is not on the job (in Zion), and therefore whether they should not expect rescue, but God interrupts with his own abrupt question: "Why have they provoked me to anger with their graven images?"

A word should be said about 9:1-2. In verse 1 we have an affecting utterance of Jeremiah's, a passage which has given rise to the description of Jeremiah as the "weeping prophet":

> O that my head were waters,
>   and my eyes a fountain of tears,
> that I might weep day and night
>   for the slain of the daughter of my people!

In verse 2 we have a contrasting utterance, in which the speaker wishes to be off in the desert away from his people. The commentators have assumed that the speaker in verse 2 is also Jeremiah, but it seems clear that verse 2 is spoken by *God* (verse 3 continues the utterance, and the commentators are then forced to emend the text to avoid "and they do not know me," plainly uttered by God; further, there is a passage with similar wording in 14:8, where the people call God a "wayfarer" in language quite close to 9:2). What has happened here is that God is sarcastically mimicking Jeremiah: Jeremiah wishes his head could gush water for his people; good, but God says by contrast that *he* wishes he were off in the desert alone, far away from his people. We are a long way from the liberating God who brought his faithful people through the fearful desert and out of it again as an act of grace (2:6)!

The *Revised Standard Version* and other translations have misunderstood the grammar and imagery of verse 3. The Hebrew reads:

> They stretch their tongue,
>   their bow is a lie,
> and not for truth
>   are they strong in the land.

56

The tongue is not the bow, as the translations would have it; the "lie" is the bow that shoots the tongue (like an arrow) out to do its damage (indeed, verse 8 says explicity that the tongue is the arrow). Jeremiah's image is much stronger than our mistranslation would indicate.

In verse 4 there is a pun on the name Jacob. Jacob supplanted Esau in the old story of their birth (Genesis 25:26). Jeremiah is saying, Everyone is a Jacob these days, tricking his brother.

Notice, finally, that 9:9 concludes with the same refrain with which 5:9 and 5:29, earlier sections, were concluded. We are on familiar territory.

The section 9:17-22 spells out in detail what is involved in community lament, that which Jeremiah appealed to the people to undertake (4:8, 6:26); the people are told to summon the professional funeral women to come and prepare for the funeral of the people. The term here in Hebrew, *hakāmāh* (literally, "wise woman"), refers to one who is gifted at leading the community in the dirge, tearing her hair and baring her breast and singing the laments that the occasion demands. (It is curious that a similar phrase in French, *sage-femme,* again literally "wise woman," means "midwife.") The content of the dirge which the professional funeral women are to sing is found in verses 21-22 (again, the conjunction "for" is erroneous, as in 4:8 and 6:26; and note also that the words "Speak, 'Thus says the Lord'" at the beginning of verse 22 are unoriginal, added later in the process of formation of the book). Verse 22 ends with a horrifying image: it is not simply the distasteful comparison of the Israelites falling on the field of battle with falling dung, but more particularly it is that this word for the Israelites is a word that once was pronounced by the prophet Elijah for Queen Jezebel (2 Kings 9:37). Queen Jezebel had been the protagonist of Baal worship in the northern kingdom more than two centuries before, and she typified all that was against devotion to Yahweh; now, Jeremiah says by quoting the old phrase, the whole people is worthy of the name of the scorned queen.

The last section (10:17-25) begins with God's word to the people under battle siege (verses 17-18); the people respond with "Woe is me" (verses 19-20) as they have before (4:31); Jeremiah reports on the continuing stupidity of the leaders (verse 21)— "shepherds" is evidently a metaphor for "prophets," whose task

57

it is to "inquire of the Lord" (compare 21:7, 2 Kings 22:13-14, and many other passages)—and God once more (verse 22) alludes to the foe from the north and speaks of a great "commotion." Unfortunately that English word does not carry the strength which the Hebrew word does; the same Hebrew word is used of the "earthquake" in 1 Kings 19:11. "Uproar" might be better.

The chapter ends with verses 23-25, which have been misunderstood by the commentators in several ways. The words are spoken not by Jeremiah but by the people. The people speak in the singular, as they have earlier (for example, "Woe is me," verse 19). The people are saying, in effect, God, you keep asking us to walk rightly (6:16), but we are not really responsible (they seem to be mimicking conventional wisdom, quoting Proverbs 16:9!). If you are going to punish us at all, do it modestly and within reason, so that you do not wipe us out altogether ("bring me to nothing")—after all, you promised our father Abraham, did you not, that we would become as numerous as the stars of the heavens (Genesis 15:5)?—and a promise is a promise. If you wish to express your anger on a grand scale, why not do it against those pagan nations which do not even acknowledge your sovereignty (verse 25)? And here Jeremiah has the people quote Psalm 79:6-7, a prime example of narrow nationalism within the hymn collection of the people: "because those nations are eating up Jacob" is the way verse 7 of the psalm begins—back to the old assumptions by which God would punish the nations that "eat" Israel (2:3)! Jeremiah could not have chosen a more cunning way to depict the fatuous and uncomprehending sensibilities of the people. They will never learn. "Punishment, yes, but nothing thoroughgoing, please; a wrist tap, if you must, God; but save your energy for your old tasks of leading us in holy war."

Such is the message of God's action, his declaration of war on his own people.

Let us look back now. The seven sections of material in chapters 4-6, together with the three further sections in chapters 8-10, make up in their totality a terrible picture of disaster. The material we have examined is broken, in the present arrangement of the book of Jeremiah, by several interruptions. There is the prose passage 7:1—8:3, which we shall consider in chapter V, and the long poem against idolatry, 10:1-16, which may or may not be genuine to Jeremiah, but in either case hardly belongs in the present sequence of poems. There are other, shorter patches of nonoriginal material—5:18-19, 9:12-16, 9:23-26—which may or may not reflect tradition from Jeremiah at several steps removed from his own words. We have also skipped by several sections of genuine material too—we have hardly looked at the prelude (4:1-4) and postlude (8:4-10a and 13) and have omitted altogether any consideration of short items like 5:30-31 and 9:10-11—but it is hoped the reader has gained a firm enough grasp on Jeremiah's message by now that these passages can be read without further help.

There had never been war poetry quite like this in the Israelite tradition, and part of the reason is the device of dialogue upon which we have already commented. There had been earlier descriptions of battle—early battle songs such as that found in Judges 5, even prophetic oracles describing the inexorable march of the foreign invader (we referred briefly at the beginning of the present chapter to Isaiah 5:26-30); there had been gloating descriptions of the fall of the capital of the hated and feared Assyrians, the great city of Nineveh (the book of Nahum), and even a poem reflecting the paralysis of the Israelites when the "Chaldeans" (Babylonians) come down upon them (Habakkuk 1). But the liveliness and variety of effects which Jeremiah produces is something new: we hear the trumpet, we feel the panic of the leaders, we hear the laments of the people, we sense the emotion of the prophet, we even hear the battle cry of the enemy; and over it all we have the steady explanations from God. This is new and really quite stunning. No wonder Jeremiah's hearers reacted so strongly.

For they did react, we must not forget it. We have been putting so much of our attention in this chapter to explaining the ideas and images of these poems that we need to stop and affirm how surprising and unwelcome and unpopular these poems would be. We tend to assume when we think about the Old Testament that the religious outlook of Israel was fairly nationalistic, and in this assumption is a large amount of truth. Israel, like any other people, would tend to assume that she herself, Israel, was the center of the universe. And since we ourselves believe we have outgrown such narrow views, we assume that we may bypass the

Old Testament (except, of course, for a few well-worn passages like the twenty-third Psalm) in favor of a more universalistic faith.

But not all the Old Testament reflects such nationalistic feelings by any means, and Jeremiah's poems are a prime example. What kind of religious thinking is this, what kind of God is this, about which we have been reading in these poems? God declaring war on his own people—what would lead *this* affirmation to be incorporated into Israel's story? Now there was background before Jeremiah for a challenge to narrow nationalism. Amos had proclaimed this word from God to Israel: "You only have I known of all the families of the earth; therefore I will punish you for all your iniquities (Amos 3:2)," and, at another point: "Are you not like the Ethiopians to me, O people of Israel (Amos 9:7)?" And Isaiah had affirmed that God was sending Assyria ("the rod of [God's] anger") against his own people Israel, whom he called "godless" (Isaiah 10:5-6). Indeed, every prophetic judgment on the people is in some way a rebuke to the comfortable assumption that God simply favored his own people.

Punish, yes; but destroy? Destroy the people; nay, destroy all creation? These visions far exceed anything that earlier prophets even in their criticism of Israel's nationalism had voiced; monstrous visions, indeed. And, mind you, this declaration of war and destruction was to issue, said Jeremiah, from the hand of the God who was at the same time *brokenhearted* over the unfaithfulness of his beloved people. How can we square the brokenhearted God with the God who wars on the people he has loved into being?

It is not easy to square these, but let us think in the direction of an answer. First, the real opposite of loving and caring is not hating but rather not-caring: it is indifference. God was never indifferent to his people. If they ruined his experiment in intentional community, he would have to take steps.

Let us try a modest little parable. Let us imagine a doctor who is determined to find a cure for cancer. To this end he builds a laboratory and builds up a population of several thousand mice for his experiments. He has bred these mice, he has worked with them, and he has waited patiently, generation by generation, for the strains to develop which he needs. Then suppose, in a way analogous to the story in George Orwell's book *Animal Farm*, [3]

60

that one weekend the mice decide to take matters into their own hands. They find a way to escape from their cages, they cross-breed, they destroy the cell cultures that the doctor has developed, and when the doctor returns on Monday morning the mice are well on their way to devising a scheme for escaping from the laboratory altogether. What is the doctor to do? Does he dust off his hands, give up, turn his back on the goal to seek a cancer cure? Or does he not rather, sorrowfully, gather up the mice, exterminate them, and begin all his painful, careful experimentation from scratch? This is perhaps a dim analogy to the vision which Jeremiah had of God at work.

And the curious thing is that Jeremiah's anticipation of destruction came true: when Jerusalem fell in 587 B.C., the city became virtually uninhabitable. There was a shortage of food and water (Lamentations 4:4, 9), and people even resorted on occasion to cannibalism (Lamentations 4:10). The people who were undergoing these horrors searched frantically for an explanation, and Jeremiah's was the only one at hand that really made any sense. What Jeremiah had done was to offer them a theology for disaster before the disaster struck. Few heeded his warnings when they were first uttered, but after the disaster came, hindsight would encourage them to begin to reflect on his words, words which became more and more precious as the tragedies of the people multiplied.

It must be said, of course, that destruction was not the sole message that Jeremiah would have to offer; his task was "to build and to plant" as well as "to uproot and to smash" (1:10). There would be hope, and we shall see the shape of that hope in chapter VIII. But we must not leap to the hope too quickly; we must stay awhile with the question as to what it could mean, really, for a God to turn against his own beloved people.

Chapter V

A Sermon, a Scroll, and a Scribe

We turn now to two incidents which took place early in Jeremiah's career (if our chronology is correct; at least we can be sure that they took place early in the reign of Jehoiakim). The two incidents are the preaching of the sermon at the Temple (chapters 7 and 26) and the dictating of a scroll to the scribe Baruch (chapter 36). Both incidents have been referred to briefly, toward the end of chapter II, but we must take a closer look at them.

The long prose section 7:1—8:3 interrupts the sequence of poems concerned with the foe from the north; we shall see in a moment why it seems to have been placed here. But it is in an altogether different style: we no longer have the clipped, compact, poetic lines in parallelism with each other, but instead an expansive, repetitive sort of prose material—in short, a sermonic style. Jeremiah is bidden to stand in the gate of the Lord's house (7:2) and speak out a message. A climax of this message is the mention of Shiloh (verses 12 and 14). In chapter 26 we evidently have a parallel account of the delivery of this sermon, though there the account centers not on the words but on the events that accompanied the words, for there we are told that at the beginning of the reign of Jehoiakim (who began to reign, we recall, in 609 B.C.) Jeremiah is to stand in the court of the Lord's house (26:2) and speak out a message, and the climax of this message is the mention of Shiloh (verses 6 and 9).

There are four related questions with which we must deal at the beginning. First of all, does this so-called Temple Sermon take up all of 7:1—8:3 or only a part of it, and, if only a part, then how much of it? A close look at this section reveals it to be a chain of five sections of prose (verses 3-15, climaxed by "Shiloh"; verses 16-19, a command to Jeremiah not to intercede for his people; verse 20, on God's destruction; verses 21-34, material on false worship; and 8:1-3, a kind of appendix). This material seems to be linked together by the repetition of the word "place," repeated eight times in the course of the whole passage. In short, we have here a *collection* of prose material, and I rather suspect that only 7:3-15 should be called the Temple Sermon proper.

Second, are we to take the words of this sermon as word-for-word recording of the sermon, from beginning to end, as we assume the poetry of the earlier chapters to have been word for word what Jeremiah uttered? I think not. Poetry and prose function quite differently in a culture, particularly in a culture which centers around speaking rather than writing. Think of the difficulty of recording any dictated words in the days before the invention of shorthand (to say nothing of tape recorders!). A poem *can* be dictated, word for word; a poem has its own inner structure, its own rhythm and balance. In a poem, every word has its place. But prose, spoken at normal speed, can hardly be recorded as it was uttered. The best that can be expected is a gist of what was said, and that gist will inevitably depend upon the writing habits, the stylistic habits, of the scribe. Later in this chapter of our study we shall meet Jeremiah's scribe Baruch. For now, I think we can assume that it was he who recorded Jeremiah's Temple Sermon too. Perhaps he set it down years later, long after the event. I think this contrast between poetry and prose, and the difficulty of recording prose word for word, and the inevitable participation of the scribe's writing habits, explains the startling contrast in style between the poetry we have been studying and this prose.

A third question then comes up: If Jeremiah delivered a sermon in prose on the steps of the Temple, what are the situations in which he would have delivered his poetry? The answer, I am afraid, is that we just do not know. There is a good deal of evidence that the prophets were ecstatics—that is, that they uttered their poetic oracles while in a trance or semitrance state. This evidence is hard to fit together but is suggestive: the verb "to prophesy" in Hebrew also means "to rave" (compare, for example, the translation of 1 Samuel 18:10 in the *King James Version*—Saul "prophesied"—with the translation in the *Revised Standard Version*—Saul "raved"). Jeremiah himself speaks of the prophets as running (23:21) and of saying, "I have dreamed, I have dreamed" (23:25). One has the impression that the prophets uttered their oracles while in an abnormal psychological state; in any event, the contrast between the poetry attributed to Jeremiah and the prose attributed to him is very keen.

A fourth question, now: Why is this section of prose placed *here* in the book of Jeremiah? The answer, I think, is that "burnt offerings and sacrifices" are mentioned in 7:21 and 22, twice, and this association of words meant that the section of prose was filed into the poetic material as soon as convenient after 6:20, where a poetic sequence likewise mentions "burnt offerings" and "sacrifices." This kind of word association was the means by which the growing collection of material pertaining to Jeremiah was built up; it is confusing to the modern reader but made sense to the ancient collector.

Now let us turn to the thrust of Jeremiah's sermon. What was he saying? It is quite obvious; this prose does not need much commentary! God says, Change your ways, and I will let you dwell here (verse 3); do not complacently assume the absolute security of the Temple (verse 4). If you really adhere to the Ten Commandments (verse 6), then all will be well; but if you continue to break them (verse 9), you have no right to assume that you can come to the Temple and expect me to rescue you (verse 10). We are struck by the "den of robbers" phrase in verse 11; obviously Jesus was thoroughly familiar with this material (see Mark 11:17). And then we have the comparison with Shiloh (verses 12, 14) and the threat to make Jerusalem like Shiloh. The words are plain, but much lies behind them.

The first thing we must understand is that the prophet Isaiah seems to have staked his reputation a hundred years before on the inviolability of the city of Jerusalem: read Isaiah 31:4-5 or 37:33-35. According to the tradition about Isaiah, he insisted that though the invader might trample across Judah, might shut up the soldiers of Judah in Jerusalem "like a bird in a cage" (so the oft-quoted inscription of the Assyrian King Sennacherib), nevertheless Jerusalem would not fall.[1] Now since, as a matter of

64

fact, Jerusalem did not fall under the heel of Sennacherib, the prestige of Isaiah (and of Jerusalem!) stayed high. What a marvelous sense of security this conviction would give: when an invader marched, all one had to do was to get inside the walls of Jerusalem and stay there!

This conviction of the inviolability of Jerusalem was reinforced by the confidence which the people had in Jeremiah's day that they had done their part in God's sight by destroying the outlying altars and centralizing all sacrifice at the Temple in Jerusalem, as they had done in the reform sponsored by King Josiah (see chapter II). The pendulum evidently swung back after Josiah's death, and some measure of Baal worship was tolerated (7:9 says so), but there is no evidence that altars to Yahweh were ever reestablished outside Jerusalem in this period. No, the Deuteronomic scroll had indicated that worship was to be centralized (Deuteronomy 12:5-6) in the one place which the Lord would indicate; and it was assumed that that place was obviously Jerusalem (compare 2 Kings 23:9). The reform had been carried out, at least to that extent; no wonder the people were confident, the religious establishment particularly.

Religious establishments are almost inevitably tempted into complacency, into a feeling that they have done their part for God and therefore that God will do his part for them. They know the tradition, after all; they know how worship is to be carried on; they know what God expects of them and of the world. And, knowing the standard operating procedure, they carry it out. And since God has fulfilled his promises before, they see no reason to suspect that he will not continue as he has in the past. "This is the temple of the Lord, the temple of the Lord, the temple of the Lord" (7:4).

Jeremiah, then, was faced with the twin traditions from Isaiah and from Deuteronomy, the one affirming that Jerusalem would never be taken, the other affirming that worship in Jerusalem was what God expected. (When did this confrontation between Jeremiah and the authorities take place, 609 b.c.? So how old was he then by our reckoning, eighteen years old? No wonder Jeremiah had hesitated to accept his call.)

He challenged the authorities on the basis of the only kind of argumentation which had any chance of communicating: on the basis of historical experience. He mentioned Shiloh. This was probably in very poor taste, as we say; there was a kind of conspiracy of silence about what had happened to Shiloh, as there was to be later on about the death of Josiah.[2] What was it that had happened at Shiloh, and why would Jeremiah bring it up at this point?

We have already had occasion to refer to Shiloh at the beginning of chapter II; it had been the central sanctuary of the Israelites in the early days, where Samuel grew up, and we have seen how the village of Anathoth may have preserved its old traditions. Now after Samuel reached adulthood, the enemy Philistines from the west came in and took Shiloh, captured the sacred Ark of the Covenant which had symbolized God's presence with the Israelite army, and then evidently destroyed the sanctuary there (compare 1 Samuel 4). The Israelites eventually regained possession of the Ark of the Covenant—the Philistines were superstitiously fearful of its power (1 Samuel 5:6-12)—but Shiloh never again became a sanctuary for the Israelites. There is no account in 1 Samuel of the burning of Shiloh (was the event too painful to be remembered?), and only one other passage even indirectly indicates what had happened: we read in Psalm 78:60, "He [God] forsook his dwelling at Shiloh, the tent where he dwelt among men."

Jeremiah's message is plain: God does not *need* the Temple at Jerusalem, any more than he needed the sanctuary at Shiloh; he uses the Jerusalem Temple so long as the worshipers there really adhere to his expectations, but he does not need the structure. Indeed, he is perfectly capable of burning down the Temple as he burned down his former sanctuary at Shiloh. But, one might ask, what about the "gospel according to Isaiah," the good news that Jerusalem is inviolable? The answer that Jeremiah would give is that God is not bound by his earlier behavior; *God can change his mind*. He decided to save Jerusalem in Isaiah's day; he has decided now to destroy Jerusalem. Who knows, he might change his mind once more and save the city, if Israel changes her ways (26:3, 13)! This sense of a free-lance God, a God not bound by any habits in the past, must have been an appalling message to speak out to the religious establishment of Jerusalem, bound as they were by a careful adherence to the habits and procedures of the past.

Bound in with this vision of a free-lance God is the corollary:

cultic observances, the proper sacrifices, are not *sufficient* to please God. They may be necessary, part of the given of God's expectations, but they are never sufficient. In this Jeremiah was only echoing what earlier prophets had pronounced (compare Amos 5:21-24 and Isaiah 1:12-17 among many such passages). Worship unaccompanied by deeds is empty (7:10). It is easy to make this affirmation but hard to remember it.

The reaction of the authorities to this sermon is worth examining (26:7-24). It was of course the religious authorities who first heard him ("the priests and the prophets," verse 7). What did they object to? According to verse 9, it was Jeremiah's reference to the destruction both of the Temple and of the city that caught their attention. According to the record, they called the civil authorities over from the palace ("the princes," verses 10 and 11) and reported Jeremiah's speech to them. Is this only a casual abbreviation of the narrative which we read here, or is it significant that when they repeated the offending words, they omitted the reference to the Temple and spoke only of Jeremiah's prophesying against the city (verse 11)? This would suggest treason rather than a religious squabble. Jeremiah's defense before the civil authorities was quite simple: Do as you wish with me. But you must understand that I do not speak for myself; I am a spokesman for God—it is he who sent me. So if you execute me, you will be calling God's anger down upon yourselves and upon the city for which you are responsible (verses 12-15).

This statement cut through to the religious fears of the princes, and they found the complaint of the religious leadership unconvincing. The princes accordingly turned the matter back to the religious authorities, saying, in effect, This does not concern us, it is in your department: after all, the man speaks for God (verse 16).

An elder broke the impasse: as Jeremiah had cited Shiloh as a precedent, the elder cited a precedent for the situation they were in. The prophet Micah over a hundred years before, he pointed out, had similarly prophesied the destruction of both the Temple area and the city (verses 17-18; the passage is to be found in Micah 3:12), and King Hezekiah did not put *him* to death. True enough; and this precedent was enough to save Jeremiah's life. But the king would not be pleased by Jeremiah's sermon, and the narrative adds an account (verses 20-23) of another prophet whose message was similar to that of Jeremiah, the prophet Uriah. The king tried to kill Uriah, but Uriah escaped to Egypt; the king, however, sent a posse and captured him and brought him back to the king, who executed him and threw his body in the community burying ground. Let Jeremiah be warned! It was fortunate that Jeremiah had a friend at court (verse 24).

Was this Temple Sermon the very first public event of Jeremiah's career? We have tended to this assumption (see again the discussion in chapter II). If so, one can only sense that Jeremiah is, to put it facetiously, off to a great start. Sometime later we are told that he was "debarred" from going to the Temple (36:5, in 605 b.c.), and this prohibition quite likely had its inception at the time of the Temple Sermon. The opposition to Jeremiah grew—we shall see another example of it in the second incident to be examined, the incident of the scroll, and we shall study the pattern of opposition to Jeremiah more thoroughly in chapter VI.

But let us pause to ponder the whole matter of prophecy misunderstood as blasphemy or treason, or both. Jeremiah walked the way that countless others since his time have walked: one thinks of Socrates and Jesus and so many others, who are called subversive and are threatened with death, who are sentenced to death and the sentence passed, all because they dared to question the eternal verities. Those who live in later decades and later centuries may see clearly how the words of a fresh thinker have been vindicated by subsequent events, but such second-guessing does not necessarily lead to greater wisdom when another fresh thinker comes along. It was peculiarly difficult for Jeremiah's peers to understand how God might level a judgmental word against the religious establishment, for of course the whole experiment of monarchy in Israel and Judah had reinforced an identification between church and state, to use current terms. Once a nationalistic enterprise is deemed sacred, once a nation-state is understood to be the expression of the will of God, it seems to be peculiarly difficult for people to accept any challenge to the system. Jeremiah was forced to take account of the issue, in his day, as to whether "church" needed to be "state" as well, and whether either could be identified with the will of God. Public reaction was quick and stiff.

But before we leave chapter 7 of the book of Jeremiah, we

should perhaps say a word about the meaning of 7:16, in which God bids Jeremiah not to pray for the people to God. Traditionally it was one of the tasks of the prophet to intercede to God for the people. Amos interceded for the people in his day (Amos 7:2, 5), and Isaiah was asked by the courtiers of King Hezekiah to pray to God for the people (2 Kings 19:4). There are indications in the material of Jeremiah that he, too, prayed to God on behalf of the people, not only indirect reflections such as we found in 9:1 but quite clearly in a passage like 18:20: "Remember how I stood before thee to speak good for them, to turn away thy wrath from them." But according to 15:1, even those great intercessors of the far past, Moses and Samuel, would at this point be of no avail. And now here in 7:16 one has the same message, bluntly stated. How can one reconcile such absolutes? Is Jeremiah to pray for his people or not, and if not, why not?

It must be admitted that the language of the Old Testament is of the all-or-nothing-at-all variety. Things are either black or white, good or bad. Thus in Genesis 29:31 we read that Leah was "hated." We have no evidence that her husband, Jacob, wanted her out of the way, only abundant evidence that he preferred his other wife, Rachel. But for the Old Testament there is no more or less to loving, only "loving" and "hating." (When Jesus speaks of "hating" God and "loving" Mammon, or vice versa [Matthew 6:24], is he not also talking about priorities? And what about "hating" father, mother, wife, and children [Luke 14:26]? Matthew has understood that saying rightly [Matthew 10:37]!) So with praying for the people: the Israelite had no middle ground, no way to talk about ambivalence. At a given moment God either accepted or rejected a prophet's prayers on behalf of the people. The appalling thing is not the inconsistency—shall I or shan't I?—but the simple sense that it is too late for any prayers to avail.

We turn now to the second incident which occurred early in Jeremiah's career, his dictation of a scroll in the fourth year of Jehoiakim (605 B.C.); the narrative is found in chapter 36. The whole chapter reads smoothly and understandably, and the reader is urged to read it through. God told Jeremiah to dictate a scroll of his words of judgment, and so he did; he called the scribe Baruch and dictated "all the words of the Lord which he had

69

spoken to him" (verse 4). Since Jeremiah was debarred from going to the Temple himself (verse 5), he used this means of communicating God's words to the people when they were assembled for a public fast. When the authorities heard of it, they took Baruch off immediately to the palace. One has a kind of feeling of "Here we go again"; there are the same old cronies— one notes the presence at court of Elnathan the son of Achbor, who had headed the posse to Egypt to bring back the prophet Uriah for execution (36:12; compare 26:22). When the courtiers heard the scroll read to them by Baruch, their immediate reaction was that the king must hear of it. Where, they asked, did Baruch get the scroll? Was it at "his" dictation? (verse 17). (Were they averse to speaking the name of Jeremiah?) It was, said Baruch. Go and hide, they said, and let no one know where you are (verse 19). When a court official then read out the scroll to the king, the king simply cut it up, piece by piece, and tossed it into the fire (verse 23); we have already dealt with this incident as an indication of the king's wish to rid the land of the effect of the words of the scroll (chapter II). Even Elnathan (he of the posse) urged the king not to destroy it, but the king would not listen (verse 25). This time the king ordered both Baruch and Jeremiah to be seized, but fortunately they eluded capture (verse 26). The upshot of all this was that Jeremiah was bidden by God to dictate the contents of the first scroll once more, on a fresh scroll; he did, adding further words (verse 32) and giving voice to a curse against the king as well (verses 30-31).

This event raises many questions in our minds. To the question of why Jeremiah would be impelled to dictate a scroll, there are two immediate answers in the narrative itself. The theological answer is that God bade him to (verse 2), and the circumstantial answer is that it was a way to communicate with the populace since the prophet himself is forbidden to come personally (verse 5).

But there may be another factor at work. It may not be apparent to the modern reader, accustomed as he or she is to a world filled with printing and writing of all sorts, but in Jeremiah's day the idea of a prophetic scroll was unprecedented.

Jeremiah grew up in a world of speaking and hearing, not of writing and reading. There are only a handful of inscriptions and other written material that have been dug up in Palestine, in strong contrast to the libraries of written material from ancient Egypt and Assyria and Babylonia. People committed really important material to memory in those days, and memorization was as prized then as it is among Arabs and others in the MIddle East today. No earlier prophet wrote down his material or dictated his material, as far as our evidence goes;[3] the prophets spoke out their words, had their words committed to memory, and only much later did disciples or collectors begin to make written material of them.

The one great precedent for Jeremiah's scroll is of course the scroll discovered in the Temple in 621 B.C. which served as a basis for the reform of King Josiah, that scroll which was evidently the core of the book of Deuteronomy (see chapter II). We do not know the origin of that scroll; some scholars think it had its origin in northern circles of Levitical priests who brought their lore south with them as refugees after the collapse of the northern kingdom in 721 B.C.[4] If this is so, it would suggest that the Israelites resorted to writing only when the living oral tradition was in danger of being lost because of social disarray: if a nation collapsed, if the tradition-bearers were to be scattered, then writing must come to the rescue.

This scroll of Deuteronomy purported to be the words of Moses to Israel, and the discovery of the scroll in the Temple meant virtually a rediscovery of Moses for the people of the kingdom of Judah in 621 B.C. and after. We have already seen that Jeremiah saw himself as the prophet like Moses in carrying on the tradition of Moses in a fresh way to the people after the death of Josiah in 609 B.C. Now so long as the prophet himself is alive and well, so long as there is social continuity and hearers can heed and remember, then all is well; so Jeremiah spoke his oracles.

But suppose Jeremiah's life is in danger? Suppose Jeremiah himself has no sons to carry on his work (compare 16:2)? Suppose Jeremiah is keenly aware of the coming collapse of the nation and all the fabric of its society? What then? Then resort to a scroll; and since Jeremiah could not necessarily write, or at least write easily, he engaged a scribe, Baruch.

The whole narrative of chapter 36 is an almost perfect replication of the narrative in 2 Kings 22:3—23:3 of the finding and the publishing of the Deuteronomic scroll, down to some of the personnel involved: Shaphan the secretary was involved with

71

the first scroll (2 Kings 22:3), Gemariah the son of Shaphan with Jeremiah's scroll (36:10, 12); we have met Elnathan the son of Achbor (36:12; compare 26:22), but Achbor his father figured in the narrative of the first scroll (2 Kings 22:12). To us the whole business seems artificial, but really there is no reason to doubt either historical account. However, one does become aware that the writer of chapter 36 (presumably Baruch) wanted to underline the similarity of the process by which the two scrolls came to public attention.

Jeremiah's dictation of the scroll, then, not only underlines the contention that he saw himself to be the prophet like Moses but also the fact that it was a risky time for a prophet to carry on his ministry; committing to a scroll the words that had come from God was not only a precaution but a very extreme one![5]

These first tasks of dictation were the beginning of a long association between Jeremiah and Baruch. Seventeen years later, on the eve of the final fall of Jerusalem, Jeremiah would entrust Baruch with the preservation of the title-deed to a field which the prophet had redeemed (32:13, 16)—we shall take account of that incident in chapter VIII—and then, after the fall of Jerusalem, when Jeremiah became involved with a group of refugees going down to Egypt, Baruch would accompany him (43:6). And one has the impression that during this period Baruch was busy setting down the words and deeds of Jeremiah, and that it was he who was largely responsible for the shape and extent of the book of Jeremiah as we now have it. We shall return to this matter at the end of chapter IX.

At the beginning of the association, in 605 B.C., Baruch quickly found himself in trouble; the king had a warrant out for Baruch's arrest as well as for Jeremiah's (36:26). Modest man that he was, he allowed himself in the book of Jeremiah only one small passage where we learn of his reactions as well (chapter 45, a short passage of only five verses). As Jeremiah will say, "Woe is me" (15:10), so does Baruch (45:3):

> Woe is me!
>   for the Lord has added sorrow to my pain;
> I am weary with my groaning,
>   and I find no rest.

But God has a word for him too, and it is a word that picks up the four verbs of Jeremiah's call in 1:10:

> Behold, what I have built I am breaking down,
> And what I have planted I am plucking up.

The verbs "to build" and "to plant" in 1:10 evidently refer to new hope after disaster, but in the word to Baruch they are used of the original hopes and plans of God for his community. But beyond the general disaster which has to come, this word:

> And do you seek great things for yourself?
> Seek them not;
> For behold, I am bringing evil upon all flesh . . .;
> But I will give your life as a prize of war
> in all places to which you may go.

No great expectations, please, Baruch; be grateful for small favors; in the swirl of persecution and war which is about to swallow us up you can snatch one bit of plunder—your own life. It is all you may expect; do not despise a day of small things (compare Zechariah 4:10!).

For folk who had been told for years that God rewards faithful people and punishes unfaithful ones (compare Deuteronomy 28:1-6 and 15-19, or 30:15-18, or Psalm 1; there are countless passages like these in the Old Testament), it was a bewildering time. And for Jeremiah, at least, worse was yet to come.

Chapter VI

The People Against Jeremiah

Jeremiah aroused the enmity of King Jehoiakim in the first four years of his reign; we have learned in chapter V how Jeremiah preached a sermon in the Temple and then dictated a scroll of his words of judgment, so that his life and the life of his scribe Baruch were threatened. And we took note of the curse from God which Jeremiah leveled at the king after the king had burned his scroll (36:29-31). Indeed, Jeremiah was quite convinced that God held the king in low repute; we have another sequence of material, this time in poetry, that announces God's judgment upon Jehoiakim (22:13-19). We gather from this passage that the king had undertaken some renovation of the palace and used forced labor of his citizenry to accomplish it (verses 13-14), and the oracle compares him unfavorably with his father, Josiah, in whose reign there was justice and righteousness (verses 15-17). The judgment on the king, then, is for death without proper funeral rites or burial (verses 18-19). The evidence indicates, by the way, that this particular prediction did not come true (compare 2 Kings 24:6), but such an inconsistency did not bother either the prophets or the collectors of prophetic oracles. A prophet spoke "for instances" of what God had in mind at a particular time, but he never assumed that the future was absolutely preset (compare 26:3).

The opposition to Jeremiah was not confined to the court of Jehoiakim, however, and we will turn in this chapter to several vignettes in Jeremiah's career which indicate the range of opposition to him. The first emerges from the material found in 11:18—12:6. This passage is the first of the so-called "confessions" of Jeremiah, in which he gives voice to complaints against God. We shall study these passages in detail in chapter VII, postponing for now this matter of how Jeremiah came to oppose God. At present we shall simply look at the social situation that gave rise to those bitter cries.

Quite suddenly, without warning, we hear of "their" evil deeds (11:18); the text reads, "I did not know it was against me they devised schemes, saying, 'Let us destroy the tree...let us cut him off from the land of the living, that his name be remembered no more.'" Who are "they"? It becomes clear in verses 21 and 23: it is the "men of Anathoth," who "seek your life." His fellow villagers want to kill him.

We have already mentioned, in chapter III, the security which the village offered to the Israelite (see the discussion there of 2:6). In such a village culture it is always taken for granted that when a villager goes off to the city he is in somewhat alien territory; in the city he hopes to be able to settle alongside any folk from his own village who have likewise moved into the city. Thus when young men from a mountain village of Lebanon today drift into Beirut in search of work, they will take a room in a part of the city frequented by those from their own area; and on weekends, or summer afternoons, they will go back to their village, their ultimate security. So if the city in the ancient Near East offered to the villager not only more excitement and scope to his life but temporary security as well during a military emergency (see chapter IV, on 4:5), still it was the village which gave to the villager his basic social and psychological security, as it has done in most of the world for thousands of years.

But Jeremiah was denied this security; he was cut off from those with whom he grew up. He could not count on any of the support system which was assumed to be universally available to someone who moved out of the accustomed rhythm of life. Jeremiah was cut off. No wonder he fled to God in dismay.

But the situation was even worse than this, as a reply from God makes clear (12:5-6); not only his fellow villagers but even his extended family, his brothers and cousins, were in hot pursuit after him. In the Hebrew text the words which hit the eye are the phrase "even they": *even they* have dealt treacherously with you.

75

We have indicated already the extent to which older people, heads of families, one's eldest brother, were in control and made the decisions (chapter II). But there is another side to the story: if your father or older brother made the decisions, by the same token your father or older brother was responsible; he would support and take care of you and protect you. This ultimate support, this last redoubt, this sense that "no matter what they do to you, we will take care of you," was likewise denied Jeremiah. The bottom had dropped out of his life. Read Leviticus 25:47-49 and catch some sense of what family solidarity meant in the ancient Near East.

I have heard of instances in the Near East in recent years when members of a family set out to kill a kinsman. Most often, tragically, it involves a young woman who is thought, rightly or wrongly, to have committed a sexual misdeed which "dishonors" the family: it is then the duty of the father or older brother to kill the woman. (The scene of the woman taken in adultery [John 8:3-6] is still being enacted in our day.) But one also hears occasionally of a Muslim from a remote village in Iran or the like who has converted to the Christian faith. Whatever his motive in doing so, he has likewise "dishonored" the family and is assumed furthermore to be a threat: he has gone over to the "enemy" and will take the secrets of the family with him; the family must therefore seek to do away with him. Of necessity he must flee elsewhere and take up a new life, must find a completely new support system.

It is with high emotions of this sort that we are dealing here. Psychically it must have been shattering to Jeremiah to learn that not only his fellow villagers but even his own kinsmen were after him, were not only turning their backs on him but were quite deliberately seeking to hurt or kill him.

Phrases referring to Jeremiah's enemies turn up again and again in the course of these "confessions": he speaks of "my persecutors" (15:15); he says in one notable instance "I sat alone" (15:17). Perhaps it is worth our while to linger a moment with that phrase "I sat alone" and do some word study. The verb sit in Hebrew can also mean "dwell, reside"; in the Hebrew mind the verb evidently described the general action of settling down, and a person can either settle down in a chair, to sit, or settle down in a region, to stay and reside. So the translation of *The*

Jerusalem Bible for 15:17 straddles both meanings; it renders the phrase, "I held myself aloof." Now the only significant earlier use of this verb together with the word "alone" is to be found in Leviticus 13:46, the law for lepers. Read the whole passage, Leviticus 13:45-46. The leper was to "dwell alone in a habitation outside the camp," an appalling thought to those in the Near East who treasure company. And now Jeremiah is indicating that he is a social leper, treated identically: an outcast.

In what way had Jeremiah broken the code of honor of village and family? By the Temple Sermon, which might have offended his father, Hilkiah? By not marrying (16:2), an abstention which would have offended everyone's conventional cultural expectations? Or was it simply everyone's shared perception that he was a troublemaker? One wonders.

Let us next turn to the confrontation between Jeremiah and the prophet Hananiah, an incident narrated in chapter 28. The background is indicated in chapter 27, and for this incident we must review our history a little more.

Nebuchadnezzar, king of Babylon, set out to continue the westward expansionist policies that Assyria had embraced earlier in the century, and the verses of 2 Kings hint at the frantic flipflops by which King Jehoiakim attempted to keep out of trouble. He had been put on the throne by the Egyptians (2 Kings 23:34), and he paid heavy tribute to the Egyptians (2 Kings 23:35); yet after the battle of Carchemish he became a vassal of Nebuchadnezzar (this is evidently the meaning of 2 Kings 24:7), only to revolt three years later (2 Kings 24:1). All this we have seen in chapter II. Now Nebuchadnezzar marched west in 598 B.C., invading Judah in Jehoiakim's eleventh year, and in the very month in which the Babylonian armies approached Jerusalem, Jehoiakim died. (Was it death by assassination? It is altogether likely because of his foolhardy rebellion against Babylon.)[1] After his death his young son, Jehoiachin, came onto the throne; he was only eighteen years old and held the throne for only three months before Nebuchadnezzar captured Jerusalem (2 Kings 24:8-12), sending off to Babylon an immense store of booty and, beyond the booty, exiling to Babylon most of the leadership of the state, beginning with King Jehoiachin and the queen mother (2 Kings 24:13-16). Nebuchadnezzar then placed on the throne of Judah Jehoiachin's uncle (thus Jehoiakim's brother), a man named Zedekiah. Now the problem for the people of Judah, aside from the humiliation of their defeat and vassalage to Babylon, was to decide who the legitimate king was. Jehoiachin was still alive (indeed, according to Babylonian accounts, he was still alive in 560 B.C., thirty-eight years later). To whom should one give allegiance, to the king in exile (granted that he is not free to rule even from abroad) or to the puppet king in Jerusalem?

By 594 B.C. there was talk among the various states in Syria and Palestine of a concerted revolt against Nebuchadnezzar; it seemed a quite plausible plan (Jeremiah 27:1, 3; 28:1). To Jeremiah such talk was foolishness; God had decreed that the enemy would destroy the nation, and so it would be. Jeremiah felt called by God at this point to go around with a yoke on his shoulder, as a permanent sign to the people that all the nations round about would have to serve Nebuchadnezzar (27:4-11). What a sight that must have been, a kind of steady show-and-tell to the people, reminding them of their humiliation, denying them any hope whatever for the years ahead. Of course there were always folk who claimed that the dark cloud would go away, people who said, "You shall not serve the king of Babylon" (27:9). But these, as we have already pointed out, were fair-weather prophets, not to be trusted (we recall our discussion of 6:14, in chapter IV, in this regard).

The prophet Hananiah emerges now as the spokesman for the fair-weather prophets. By this time the prohibition had evidently been lifted against Jeremiah's going to the Temple, for we read that it was in the Temple that this confrontation took place (28:2). Hananiah speaks in the name of the Lord: "Thus says the Lord of hosts, the God of Israel: I have broken the yoke of the king of Babylon" (28:2). Good news! Within two years God will bring back all the gold and silver goods which Nebuchadnezzar had taken from the Temple, and he will bring back the king and all the rest of the exiles (28:3-4). Good news!

Then Jeremiah steps up (he of the yoke) and says, Marvelous, if true. But earlier prophets as a rule prophesied doom, so that the tradition in which we both stand is a doom-saying tradition. If a prophet claims a word from the Lord which is something other than doom, the burden of proof is on that prophet—since he has stepped outside the tradition (verses 6-9).

Then Hananiah grabs the yoke off the shoulders of Jeremiah

78

and breaks it, a symbolic act done in the name of God. And he has a word to go with it: "Thus says the Lord: even so will I break the yoke of Nebuchadnezzar king of Babylon from the neck of all the nations within two years" (28:10-11). Hananiah has had the last word that day, and all Jeremiah can do is go his way (verse 12).

But Jeremiah becomes convinced that he is on the right track after all, for a fresh revelation comes to him from God by which he addresses Hananiah once more: "You have broken a wooden yoke, but in their place you shall get bars of iron" (verse 13; compare *The New English Bible*, that follows the Hebrew text). It is going to get worse, not better, and the word you are preaching, Hananiah, is a spurious word (verse 15). Indeed, you do not have the proper credentials: you are not "sent" by God at all (verse 15), as a proper prophet must be "sent" (compare 23:21 and 1:7), but God will "send" you—off the face of the earth! (verse 16: the verb is the same in Hebrew and is intended as a wordplay). And, the narrative adds, Hananiah did die in the very same year (verse 17).

Now, before we are tempted to hold Hananiah in too much contempt, let us ask ourselves this question: How different was Hananiah's "gospel" from Isaiah's "gospel" a hundred years before? (We have discussed Isaiah's good news about the inviolability of Jerusalem in chapter V.) Isaiah had insisted that God would never allow Jerusalem to fall or Zion to disappear; that was the good news, and it sustained the people in Isaiah's day and, when it remained true through the years, became a cornerstone for the confidence of the people in Yahweh. So how is the word of Hananiah so very different?

Indeed, what are we to make of this confrontation between Jeremiah and Hananiah, between prophet and prophet—for we notice that the narrative constantly identifies both men by the same title (verses 5, 10, 12, 15)? Many of us, I suppose, fall into the assumption that it must have been easy back in those days to learn the will of God; one had only to listen to a prophet. We assume that it is far harder nowadays, when God does not speak out so forthrightly. But is this not a misunderstanding of the situation? It has *always* been hard to learn the will of God, for there have always been men around to speak for God, some saying "light," others saying "dark." Whom do we listen to?

And it is only in the sorting-out process of later years that one can identify who has been speaking for God and who has not.

This matter of the so-called false prophets seems to have been a constant problem in Israel. Of course the prophets whose word turned out to be wrong never called themselves false prophets; no one ever stood up and said, "I am a false prophet." All of them simply said, "Thus says the Lord," as Hananiah did (28:2). And curiously enough the valid prophets (those, that is, who are valid to us, by hindsight) usually called the false prophets (again, those who are false in our reckoning) simply "prophets." Only when the problem became terribly acute did the valid prophets try to pinpoint how the false prophets had gone astray and ceased to be effective spokesmen for God. But why should the Old Testament, so much of the time, have failed to distinguish between prophet and prophet? The reason is perhaps because all prophets, both those who spoke words that turned out to be valid and those who spoke words that did not, shared common characteristics. We suspect that in many cases they were ecstatics, cultivating trance states (we have referred to this matter in chapter V). All of them claimed to speak for God, and each of them no doubt had his train of followers who took him seriously.

The first such occasion recorded in the Old Testament where self-proclaimed spokesmen for God oppose each other in counsel is an incident in the ninth century B.C., recorded in 1 Kings 22:1-38—we have already mentioned this incident in passing, in chapter IV. The king wants to know whether he will succeed in battle; his four hundred court prophets (imagine, four hundred; what a claque!) say "yes," but perhaps a little too glibly, so the king asks for the word from Micaiah. Micaiah says "no." How can this be? How can four hundred speak for God and say "yes," and one speak for God and say "no"? Micaiah's answer is that God has sent a "lying spirit" into the mouths of the four hundred to "entice," to beguile the king. This solves the problem: *both* the four hundred *and* Micaiah do speak for God; but Micaiah speaks a true word, while the four hundred speak an enticing, a beguiling word. The king's courtiers threaten Micaiah and lock him up, and to this Micaiah's only retort is, Wait and see (1 Kings 22:25).

Then in the next century, in the eighth, the prophet Micah faced a similar problem. His solution is to affirm that his op-

80

ponents are paid to speak what they speak, whereas he, Micah, is "filled with power (Micah 3:5-8)."

Jeremiah works at the problem in a variety of ways. We have seen how he appealed to tradition to reinforce his message (28:8-9). He also, in a series of bitter oracles against these prophets, offers a number of descriptions of their situation. Their ways are darkness (23:12; this recalls Micah 3:6). Their vision is from their own minds rather than from the mouth of the Lord (23:16). God has not sent them, nor have they ever stood in God's "council" to receive his words (23:21-22). In comparison with the true word, they are like straw to wheat (23:28), while Jeremiah's word is like fire (23:29; compare 5:14) or a hammer (23:29). Ultimately they prophesy "lies" (23:26, 32). This word suggests what is rootless, hollow, insubstantial, undependable.

In the situation now confronting Judah, Jeremiah has become convinced that the gospel according to Isaiah, valid at the end of the eighth century, is no longer valid at the beginning of the sixth. God can say "light" in one century and "dark" in the next; both are valid words from God. Hananiah may be faithful to the gospel according to Isaiah, but he is a hundred years too late with it. Hananiah listens to the past, but he does not listen to the God of the present.

But how are the people to be sure? Jeremiah faces Hananiah. It is eyeball to eyeball. It is Jeremiah's "word from God" against Hananiah's "word from God." And ultimately Jeremiah has no recourse except to say, as did Micaiah of old, Wait and see (28:9, 15-17). And when Hananiah does die (in final panic? one wonders), especially when Jerusalem falls, then the people are sure: Jeremiah had spoken a true word, and Hananiah a false.

(Nevertheless, a little voice in our minds may send our thoughts in an odd direction: what if? What if Nebuchadnezzar *had* died within the year, and his empire had begun to rock with power struggles in 593 B.C. rather than in 562 B.C. as it actually did? What if Hananiah had gained new faith and new followers from these developments in Babylon? And what if Jehoiachin had been led home again in triumph to Jerusalem and King Zedekiah, the puppet of Nebuchadnezzar, had been assassinated? [We may note in Jeremiah 52:31-34 that Nebuchadnezzar's successor, Evil-merodach, did allow Jehoiachin his freedom within Babylon.] What if kingship in Jerusalem had lasted for some years after

587? Perhaps Hananiah's prophetic oracles, like Jeremiah's, were very lyrical, very moving; perhaps his words instead, consistent with Isaiah's, would be revered in centuries to come. Would the Old Testament collection then include the books of Isaiah, Hananiah, and Ezekiel? Would we be studying the book of Hananiah today? Such thoughts seem wicked, unfair to the conviction you and I may have that it was Jeremiah, not Hananiah, whom God sent, but such a conviction is, after all, built up on the basis of the *experience of Israel* over the long haul. Such thoughts are at least consistent with the empirical wait-and-see attitude which Jeremiah maintained.)

The encounter with Hananiah took place well along in the kingship of Zedekiah. Six years later the end was at hand for Jerusalem and for the kingdom of Judah, and in that emergency situation King Zedekiah himself began, in a curious and ambiguous way, to seek out Jeremiah's help and counsel. And this relationship is perhaps the most surprising of all the encounters between Jeremiah and the authorities. To follow this relationship, again, we need a bit more history.

We recall that Zedekiah had been put on the throne (597 B.C.) by Nebuchadnezzar as a puppet. He seems to have been a weak-minded man, just the type of person one might expect a foreign overlord to choose to sit on the throne of a vassal state. We recall, too, that there was talk of revolt in the air by 594 B.C., but Zedekiah protested his loyalty to Nebuchadnezzar (compare 29:3).

We have the impression that the people were agitating more and more for a rebellion against Babylon. They expected to gain help from Egypt in this enterprise, and there were evidently promises made by Egypt to send an army (37:7). We have the impression, too, that the puppet king was opposed by a nobility in his court that was pro-Egyptian and that insisted on sturdy resistance to Babylon (so, evidently, the nobles mentioned in 38:1). In any event, Nebuchadnezzar sensed that Zedekiah was not able to keep Judah safe for Babylon, and Nebuchadnezzar marched once more; at the beginning of January 588 the army was at hand and began besieging Jerusalem. Sometime during the summer of that year an Egyptian army pushed northward to try to put pressure on the Babylonians, and they evidently did lift the siege temporarily, but the Egyptian army fell back and the

Babylonians pressed their advantage; the city held out until the summer of the following year, when it finally fell, in July, 587 B.C.[2] King Zedekiah slipped out from Jerusalem with the remnant of his army but got only as far as Jericho before he was captured by the Babylonians; they took him north to Hamath, in Syria, where Nebuchadnezzar had his main camp, and he and his sons were sentenced—the sons were executed and Zedekiah himself was blinded and then taken in chains to Babylon, where he died.

Now while the siege of Jerusalem was still under way, Zedekiah sent a couple of court officials to Jeremiah, including a priest named Zephaniah, to ask what was to happen: "inquire of the Lord for us, for Nebuchadnezzar . . . is making war against us; perhaps the Lord will deal with us according to all his wonderful deeds, and will make him withdraw from us" (21:1-2). How pathetic! But, after all, the priests in the Temple were singing of the wonderful works of the Lord: look at Psalm 78, and note the language of verse 4 and verses 54-55; or look at Psalm 107:6-8. Who knows? Perhaps God will do it again.

Strange, though; why did the king send a delegation to *Jeremiah* of all people? Were there not safer prophets, men in good standing at the court, who could oblige the king (compare 37:19)? Why Jeremiah? one wonders. Did it finally begin to dawn on the authorities that in such an extreme emergency the business-as-usual prophets were perhaps of little avail and that Jeremiah might, after all, be in touch with their covenant God?

Alas, the answer Jeremiah gave them was the same one he had given over and over again: Your own weapons will be to no avail (21:4), God himself has turned against the city, and Zedekiah will be given over to the enemy (verses 5-7). The only hope lies in surrender; if you surrender, your lives will be preserved (verse 9).

Then came the news in the midst of the siege that the Egyptian army was on its way, news that must have stirred people's hopes momentarily. At that point Zedekiah sent the priest Zephaniah and a third official to make of Jeremiah one very simple, sad request: "Pray for us to the Lord our God" (37:3). And again the answer: Do not get your hopes up; the Egyptian army is a false hope (verse 7); the Babylonians (the "Chaldeans," as we have explained, were the Babylonians) will not stay away (verses 8-9); even if you were to defeat the Babylonians until all that were left

83

were wounded men lying in their tents, God is still determined—they would rise up again and burn the city (verse 10).

At that point, when the Babylonians had withdrawn from the city temporarily, Jeremiah went to slip out of the city and go north toward his village to attend to some family business, but at the gate of the city he was stopped by a sentry who accused him of deserting to the Babylonian army (37:11-13); Jeremiah had, after all, counseled deserting to the enemy as the only means by which lives could be saved. He protested his innocence, but the sentry took him off to some of the nobles, who beat him and locked him up in prison (verses 14-15). One can imagine that it would not have been easy for Jeremiah to explain to the court officials who had imprisoned him that he was not anti-Judah or pro-Babylonian but pro-God, and that it was God who was anti-Judah for the moment. Many religious spokesmen have faced similar problems of communication since Jeremiah's day.

After some days Zedekiah secretly got him out and brought him to the palace to question him face to face about any fresh word from God; we have a glimpse here not only of the way in which Zedekiah and his nobility were at cross-purposes but also the way Zedekiah continued to depend upon Jeremiah for guidance. Is there any word from God? There is, says Jeremiah, the same old word: The Babylonian withdrawal does not mean a thing; you will still be handed over to the king of Babylon (verses 16-17).

But then Jeremiah asked help from the king. What have I done to offend you or your officials? he asked. And then, pressing his advantage, he asked where all the fair-weather prophets were now, the Hananiahs. Finally he requested the king to rescind the sentence of imprisonment; food, after all, was in short supply, and he was likely to be neglected and die (verses 18-20). So the king did countermand the imprisonment and committed Jeremiah to a guardhouse, where he was at least allowed a bread ration so long as the bread should last (verse 21).

Now it was the turn of the officials to challenge the king's gesture of help to Jeremiah. After all, Jeremiah was still preaching "Surrender!" So the officials went to the king and complained that Jeremiah was lowering the morale of the troops (surely a justifiable complaint), and the king, helpless when openly challenged, shrugged his shoulders and said, "Do what you like." So this time they imprisoned him by lowering him by ropes into a muddy cistern with sheer sides (38:1-6).

An "Ethiopian eunuch" named Ebed-melech got wind of Jeremiah's predicament and went to intercede with the king. (We should understand that "eunuch" here does not necessarily imply a castrated male. Because of the fact that castrated males were customarily put in charge of the king's harem, the term "eunuch" became a court title rather than a simple descriptive term. And "Ethiopian," in the Old Testament, was evidently a general term for anyone belonging to the dark-skinned Nubian peoples from what is now the extreme south of Egypt and the Sudan; such persons were often brought in as slaves from Egypt and sometimes rose in the ranks of the court. One is reminded of another "Ethiopian eunuch" in Acts 8:27-39.) This man reminded the king that those who had put Jeremiah into the cistern were evil and that the prophet would probably die there. So again, out of immediate earshot of the nobles, the king gave orders to Ebed-melech to take a party of helpers and pull Jeremiah up out of the cistern. This was done. Back went Jeremiah to the guardhouse (38:7-13).

Once more the king arranged for a secret meeting with Jeremiah, not at the palace this time but near the Temple, and this time he said he simply wanted an answer to a question. But by this time Jeremiah was so distraught that he became convinced that anything he said to the king would cost him his life, and he certainly had no confidence that the king would suddenly follow out the will of God (38:14-16). The king assured him of his good faith, and Jeremiah thereupon repeated the message he had affirmed so many times before: Surrender, and your life will be spared and the city with it; go on fighting, and the city will be destroyed and your life taken. And then—saddest note of all—the king said, I am afraid, afraid of the Jews who have already deserted to the Babylonians; I have been a halfway resister to the Babylonians, and they will make fun of me, tease me, abuse me (38:17-19). Jeremiah reassured him once again that it would not happen but gave him a vivid notion of what *would* happen if he continued to resist: he would not only be killed, but his family and harem would be given over to the Babylonians as war loot (verses 20-23). The king then begged Jeremiah not to let anyone know of their conversation; the princes might try to bribe the prophet by holding out to him a promise not to execute him if only he would divulge the substance of the conversation between himself and the king; the king suggested simply that he say that all that passed between them was a plea from Jeremiah to the king not to be sent back to the prison—the guardhouse was preferable. The stratagem worked, and the nobles allowed him to stay in the guardhouse until the city fell (verses 24-28).

Such is the sequence of conversations between Jeremiah and the wishy-washy king. We wish we understood the character of the king better, and his motivations. Of course we do not; all we can do is to piece together what we have and to notice some precedents, earlier relationships between prophets and kings which might afford some clues as to what pressed the king to embark upon these conversations.

The closest precedent is the consultation of King Hezekiah with the prophet Isaiah during the siege of Jerusalem by the Assyrians more than a hundred years before (2 Kings 19). The Assyrian commander had mocked the defenders of the city, had mocked any faith on anyone's part that Yahweh would be able to save the city (2 Kings 18), so Hezekiah in despair had sent a delegation of both court officials and priests to Isaiah to learn if he could what God had in mind; and Isaiah was able to reassure the king that the Assyrians would not succeed.

Another precedent, even earlier in history, is that consultation of King Ahab in the north with his prophets when he was contemplating a battle against the Arameans (1 Kings 22): this was the consultation at which the four hundred court prophets answered "yes" while the prophet Micaiah answered "no"; we are familiar by now with the story.

Now Zedekiah. Here is a man who owed his elevation onto the throne to the Babylonians; he was beholden to them, he was already a man with divided obligations. How does a man feel who owes his office to a dominating foreign power? He shrugs his shoulders; one has to get along, after all. Here is a man who responds to pressures: memories of the past glories of an independent Judah, the weight of a nobility which hopes to find in Egypt an answer to Babylonian imperialism. Here is a man who tries to calculate which way the wind is about to blow. Is Egypt up and Babylon down? Or is Babylon up and Egypt down? Which way shall we jump next? And as the noose draws tighter around

Jerusalem, the business-as-usual prophets seem less and less relevant, the psalm-singers of the Temple, lauding God's marvels, more and more unrealistic. He consults them, no doubt, as Ahab consulted his. But then, as Ahab did, he hedges his bets by consulting the maverick prophet Jeremiah. Who knows? Jeremiah might turn out to be an Isaiah with marvelous news from Yahweh, news that Jerusalem once more will survive a siege intact. One can always hope and try. "Pray for us to the Lord our God." It is your job. Please.

Such at least is a possible reading of these curious meetings.

But the Babylonians were not the Assyrians, Jeremiah was not Isaiah, and Zedekiah was most emphatically not Hezekiah. The king did not follow the counsel which Jeremiah had given him. How could he? He lacked even Hezekiah's forthrightness (compare 2 Kings 18:3-6), and the officialdom around him continued till the end to press the struggle against the besieging army. But it is an astonishing story nonetheless—a king who was willing in desperation to consort with the outcast prophet in the persistent if vain hope that somewhere, somehow, sometime there would be a change of heart on God's part and Jerusalem would once again emerge to gain her freedom and her dignity. If God really were to change his heart, the king certainly wanted to have the news right away. Rarely has there been a less apt disciple of a prophet, in high or low estate.

We shall save consideration of what happened to Jeremiah after the fall of the city until chapter IX. For now we must simply ponder the experience of a prophet who for a span of more than twenty years was in trouble with the authorities: after the Temple Sermon, presumably in 609 B.C., "the priests and prophets . . . laid hold of him, saying 'You shall die!' " (26:8), and in 587 B.C., just before the fall of the city, "the princes said to the king, 'Let this man be put to death' " (38:4). And all during this time he lacked the support of family and friends in his own village. So far as we know, all he had was Baruch.

But God had said, "Be not afraid of them, for I am with you to deliver you" (1:8). Was that sufficient reassurance? No. From time to time Jeremiah felt that God's rescue was more than tardy in coming, and in loneliness and bitterness and despair, he poured out his heart to God. These private cries to God we shall consider in the next chapter.

Chapter VII

Jeremiah Against God

Before we embark upon a study of Jeremiah's bill of particulars against God, we must take a closer look at Jeremiah's call to celibacy (16:1-9). We have already referred to it a time or two, but we have not yet explored it in any depth. Jeremiah is bidden, in a narrative which comes on almost like a second call, similar to that of 1:4-5, to abstain from marriage and children, as a sign that the end is really at hand: people are going to die in the land, they shall not receive proper burial, and the vultures and dogs shall feed on their corpses (16:2-4). In the same way, he is bidden to attend neither funerals nor weddings, for the time will soon come when there will be no more opportunity for the normal course of funeral and mourning rites, and when there will be no more weddings at all.

The weddings and funerals first: think of a village society once more—weddings and funerals are the great times, the high times, the memorable times, the times of great emotion. Nothing else matters so much as that these events should go properly. A bride will save for years for a wedding dress (compare 2:32); pity the orphan girl who has no family to help her with her wedding preparations! And funerals: imagine not allowing the professional funeral women to do their work (compare 9:17-22). What do children play at? At the only games worth playing, really—weddings and funerals; this, we must understand, is the presupposition of Jesus' little parable in Matthew 11:16-17. And from all this Jeremiah was to abstain. This was enough by itself to lead to his ostracism.

But the celibacy was even more of a scandal. There is no

parallel for such a call in the rest of the Old Testament; no one else undertook such a gesture. We in our time are accustomed to a celibate priesthood, accustomed to laymen and lay women who abstain from marriage, but there was no such notion in Israel.

Further, many folk today have some notion of a life after death, which fulfills earthly life and compensates for its lacks, but so far as we can tell there was no clear notion of a life after death among the Israelites. God was a God of the living, not of the dead, and one lived on in his children. Notice, for example, how God's address to Jacob in Genesis 28:14 mixes a personal address with a prediction of his children; the verbs are singular in Hebrew: "you [singular] shall spread abroad to the west and to the east and to the north and to the south"...Jacob *is* his children; Jacob gains a new name Israel (Genesis 32:28); Jacob is the *nation* Israel. The head of the family *is* his family and lives on in it. So for Jeremiah to be deprived of the opportunity for children is for Jeremiah to become extinct. No more awesome sign could be imagined. The prophet Hosea, a hundred years before, had been told to marry a prostitute as a sign that the people were going bad (Hosea 1:2). Now Jeremiah is told to marry nobody at all as a sign that the people are coming to an end. What a sign! In the eyes of his countrymen it must have been freakish, monstrous. And what it meant, of course, was that Jeremiah felt himself forced to depend entirely upon God; God was the sole support system that he had. When, therefore, Jeremiah perceived God to be neglecting him, when Jeremiah began to work out a bill of complaints against God, it was not a kind of religious hobby but a matter of life and death.

In the record, Jeremiah's outbursts against God come on quite suddenly, without any warning (11:18 and following). It is true, there are word links with what has just preceded (11:18 has the verb "know" twice, linked up with 10:23, which begins "I know"; the prose of 11:1-17, we must understand, was inserted at a later period of the formation of the book), but there is no introductory word that might warn us of the psychological and theological dynamite just ahead, only the vague note, "The Lord made it known to me and I knew; then thou didst show me their evil deeds." No explanation yet as to who "they" are or what the problem is all about. One almost has the impression that we have stumbled here on the jottings of Jeremiah's diary, inserted at this point in the book of Jeremiah. But of course it is not a diary at all in our sense—Jeremiah was a speaking man, not a writing man; nevertheless these private prayers, couched in the same poetic style as are God's words against the people recorded earlier in the book, were obviously shared with someone (Baruch, no doubt) and entered into the record. One finds poetic laments to God elsewhere in the Old Testament—Psalm 22, for example—but the likeness in Jeremiah's style between these complaints *to God* and God's complaints against his people suggests that, if God has a problem with his people, Jeremiah is convinced he has a problem with God as well. Jeremiah certainly presents his complaints in the same kind of way. We have seen already that he is concerned from time to time whether God will look after him (1:8, 11-12), and since Jeremiah has had all his immense difficulties with various human adversaries, we are now prepared for a storm.

These prayers or laments to God have traditionally been called Jeremiah's "confessions." It is not a very good term, but it is established by usage. We already had a preliminary look at the first sequence of confessions (11:18—12:6) in chapter VI, as we realized that it is Jeremiah's fellow villagers and even his own kinsfolk who are after him. Let us take a closer look, now, at the material.

Verses 18-20 of chapter 11 are quite understandable on first reading, though several comments may be made. First, a small matter: in verse 19 the word fruit is probably an incorrect translation; the Hebrew word here is evidently an old form of the word for "sap." Second, Jeremiah has an ironic intent in quoting the enemies as he does:"Let us cut him off from the land of the living, that his name be remembered no more." Because, you see, Jeremiah has been called to abstain from marriage and children (16:2), so that what the enemies are urging is what God has already accomplished by implication beforehand: one cuts off someone's name by preventing the possibility of descendants (compare David's plea to Saul, 1 Samuel 24:21). The problem then is that the enemies' wishes for Jeremiah will succeed, ultimately, because of what God has projected for him; Jeremiah only hopes that the enemies will not add insult to injury.

This brings us to the basic thrust of verse 20. Such an ut-

90

terance, as rendered here, bothers us; we tend to be repelled by people who openly want their enemies put away, particularly those who ask God to do it. Our own culture tends to repress such feelings, and those of us who are shaped by Jesus' command to turn the other cheek are particularly put off by Jeremiah's reaction.

Of course it is obvious that Jeremiah lived a long time before Jesus, and it is obvious, too, that Jesus' word to his followers seemed quite fresh and implausible (compare Matthew 18:21). But still, we find it hard to be sympathetic to Jeremiah at this point.

But I think we misunderstand Jeremiah's situation. He is not asking God's action upon his (Jeremiah's) personal enemies, as if we were to ask God's action upon neighbors of ours who let their dogs run unleashed through our rose garden. Rather he is asking God's action upon *God's* enemies. Jeremiah is not his own man; he has turned himself over to God, and when he speaks as a prophet, he is acting as God's mouthpiece. But the scoffers who want to do away with Jeremiah want to do away with God's mouthpiece; they are challenging God's sovereignty. And so Jeremiah asks God to manifest his sovereignty over these people. Indeed, our English word "vengeance" is wrong here, and this kind of phrasing has done much mischief in our Old Testament view of God. There is no vendetta, no feuding that is indicated here. The Hebrew word means "legitimate power" or "sovereignty": Jeremiah is asking that God show himself *as God* with these people; Jeremiah is asking that he be delivered from their clutches so that he may continue unscathed to speak out God's word.[1] Jeremiah is concerned about a God who is a do-nothing God, especially since he has understood God to have promised to "deliver" him (1:8).

God's answer comes in verses 22-23; there is a poetic core to these verses, though our present text has been somewhat enlarged by prose additions. The poem evidently read:

> Behold, I shall punish them;
>   Their warriors shall die by sword,
> Their sons shall die by famine,
>   And there shall be no remnant to them;

> For I shall bring evil on the men of Anathoth
> In the year of their punishment.

A message of reassurance, in short. The words which I have translated "punish" and "punishment" here are literally "visit," "visitation"—it is the action by which God squares accounts. God is keeping track, and the accounts will be squared some day soon.

The first six verses of chapter 12 bring a fresh "confession" and response from God. We must take some time with the first part of verse 1, because the existing translations do not do it justice.

On the face of it, "Righteous art thou, O Lord," is a perfectly correct translation. These same Hebrew words appear in Psalm 119:137 and are so translated there, and rightly. But the Hebrew word that comes first in the phrase may mean "innocent" as well as "righteous"—that is, it means "righteous" in an ethical context and "innocent" in a legal one. We naturally assume that to call God by the term is to call him "righteous"—it is the obvious choice of meanings—but the law-court language of the next line of the verse brings us up short and causes us to retrace our steps. The second line might be sharpened up in our translation: "when I lodge a complaint against thee." We are in the orbit of the law court now, and the first phrase of the verse evidently could serve not only in psalm-singing (as in Psalm 119:137) but also for the declaration of innocence or acquittal by the judge (compare 2 Kings 10:9, where King Jehu declares the inhabitants of the city of Jezreel innocent of the atrocity which has been committed, using the identical phrase, though of course in the plural). So we have for the first two lines of Jeremiah 12:1:

> Innocent art thou, O Lord,
> when I file a complaint against thee.

But then the third line comes, which I am persuaded has been quite misunderstood. It contains a curious Hebrew idiom which appears nowhere else in the Old Testament but in the book of Jeremiah. The clearest parallel is in 39:5: King Zedekiah has been captured at Jericho and taken to Nebuchadnezzar at Hamath, and there "he [Nebuchadnezzar] passed sentence upon him." The same idiom appears in 1:16 ("I will utter my

92

judgments against them") and 4:12 ("I...speak in judgment upon them"). Well, if the idiom means "pass judgment/sentence upon" in these other passages, why not also here in 12:1? "Yet I would pass judgment upon thee." I suppose we are afraid of a theological scandal—*Jeremiah passing judgment upon God*—but this is, so far as I can see, what the text says, and it is certainly consistent with what we have from Jeremiah elsewhere.

Jeremiah is saying, in effect: God, you have been suing Israel for breach of contract, and I am your messenger in this regard. But when I undertook to be your messenger, you obligated yourself to me to defend me, and you have not followed through on your obligation. Therefore get down from the judge's bench, move out from the prosecutor's stand, and take your place as a defendant, so that *I* may sue *you* for breach of contract. Oh, I know, you will turn out to be innocent in any lawsuit between us; nevertheless I will have my day in court—I want to pass judgment upon you.

Such language is not unique in the Old Testament; there is much in the book of Job that is similar. Job accuses God of mismanagement, and he uses law-court language to do so; note Job 9:15-16, 19-22, for example. And as we shall argue later, one of the roots of the great poem of Job does appear to be the experience and the words of Jeremiah.

Jeremiah, having indicated that he wants to pursue God in court, then gives voice to his specific complaint: "Why does the way of the wicked prosper? Why do all who are treacherous thrive? Thou plantest them, and they take root." Many people have noticed how much the wording of these lines resembles Psalm 1:3-4 ("[The righteous man] is like a tree planted by streams of water.... The wicked are not so."). Most commentators assume that Psalm 1 was written after Jeremiah's time,[2] but I shall offer evidence later in this chapter that in fact it is the other way around: Psalm 1, I contend, is earlier than Jeremiah, and Jeremiah is here offering a parody of it. The psalm suggests that good people are made strong and sturdy by God, while bad people have no stability and are soon gone with the wind. Not so, says Jeremiah, at least as far as my experience goes; it is the wicked whom God plants and who take firm root and bear fruit. And then in a surprising phrase he goes on to say, "Thou art near in their mouth and far from their heart." (Actually, instead of

93

"heart" he says "kidneys"; the *King James Version* says "reins," which is an old word in English for kidneys. The kidneys were understood to be the seat of deep concern, as we can see from Psalm 73:21.) The wicked, says Jeremiah, may talk about God, but they have no concern for him.

Why is this a surprising phrase? Because, as we saw in chapter II when we spoke of the power of the word, the Israelite took it for granted that what a man thought was what a man said, and what he said he did; and for Jeremiah to *contrast* what a man said with what he felt or planned was almost unprecedented. (The only parallels which I have noticed in the Old Testament are Psalm 28:3 and Isaiah 29:13.)

In verse 3 we are back to the wording of 11:18-20 once more: Jeremiah asks that his enemies rather than he be the sheep for the slaughter, for God knows that Jeremiah has been faithful on his part.

Verse 4 is evidently a later addition; although it is a genuine verse to Jeremiah, it breaks the continuity of the original material here.

God's answer to 12:1-3 comes in verses 5-6, and instead of the conventional answer of 11:21-23—Yes, I will punish them, eventually—we have a very surprising answer, an answer that says, essentially, Jeremiah, you have not seen anything yet; if you think you are in a bad situation now, know that it is going to get worse. To race (literally, "run") suggests the struggles he has had with the fair-weather prophets; we recall that he says elsewhere, "I did not send the prophets, yet they ran" (23:21). Running describes some kind of ecstatic action of the prophets, evidently, and the phrase here suggests that Jeremiah was being given more than a run for his money by his rival prophets. But the opposition will get worse, says God; "horses" suggests the military might of Babylonia—we recall 4:13 and 8:16. Local opposition, God seems to be saying, is modest by comparison with the opposition which is coming when the climactic battle starts. And God suggests that opposition is even in the bosom of his family; we have taken note of 12:6 already.

The next "confession" is found in 15:10-12. Unfortunately verses 11-12 have given great difficulty to the commentators;[3] since I think we are able to get light on the meaning of the

94

passage, it is worth our while to work through some of the problems which these verses offer.

Verse 10 is plain: a pathetic cry to his mother for bringing him into the world, but with the implication of regret for being called by God to be a prophet, since that call was from *before he came forth from the womb* (1:5). He is a "man of strife"; the word "strife" is the lawsuit word which has already turned up several times (in 11:20 translated by the word "cause"). Jeremiah is the victim of constant quarrels with his fellows, so much that he is quarreling now with God. "I have not lent, nor have I borrowed, yet all of them curse me"—Polonius' advice to Laertes in Shakespeare's *Hamlet* is curiously like this ("Neither a borrower, nor a lender be; / For loan oft loses both itself and friend"), but the resemblance is perhaps merely coincidental.

Now verse 11. The *Revised Standard Version*, and other translations as well, have given up on the traditional Hebrew text and have followed the ancient Greek translation instead, which differs from the Hebrew here. I prefer to follow the Hebrew after all, which begins (as one can see from the footnote in the *Revised Standard Version*), "The Lord said." Now let us set out the Hebrew text which follows quite literally, with dummy capital letters for the puzzling verbs:

> If I have not [or: surely I have] X'ed you for good,
>   if I have not [or: surely I have] Y'ed on you,
> in a time of evil and in a time of distress,
>   the enemy.

The conjunction which begins each of the first two lines is difficult, and as we see may mean either "if not" or "surely." If we take the opening of verse 11 to be "The Lord said," there is no main clause to go with "if not": the meaning then almost certainly has to be "surely."

Let us deal with the "Y" verb first. The best parallel passage is found in Isaiah 53:6, where the translation is, "And the Lord has laid on him the iniquity of us all." The wording is so close to our passage in Jeremiah that I suspect that the writer of Isaiah 53:6 (who was not the original Isaiah of Jerusalem, but another prophet who wrote after Jeremiah's lifetime) was influenced by our Jeremiah phrase. Now if the phrase in Isaiah 53:6 means, "The Lord has laid on him the iniquity of us all," then the phrase in Jeremiah 15:11 must mean, "Surely I have laid on you, in a time of evil and in a time of distress, the enemy."

The first verb, the "X" verb, will then have to have something to do with the enemy, by the pattern of poetic parallelism. There is a word that turns up frequently in the psalms, meaning "enemy"—it is found, for example, in Psalm 5:8, and is in the form of a participle. We cannot find a good participle in English which would be a synonym for "enemy"; such a word would have to mean "one who hates, one hating, a hater," or the like. Jeremiah seems to have made a straight verb out of this participle; the text fits this idea perfectly. We might then translate the verse as follows:

> The Lord said,
> > Surely I have "foe'd" you for good,
> > > surely I have laid on you,
> > in a time of evil and in a time of distress,
> > > the enemy.

So understood, God is answering Jeremiah (who of course was not really addressing his mother literally at all, but only metaphorically) and saying, As a matter of fact I know exactly what I am doing; I am fully in control. It is the same impression which we gained from God's answer in 12:5-6.

In contrast to the situation in verse 11, in verse 12 every word by itself is clear to us; it is how the words fit together that is the problem. Here are the words:

> can-break   iron   iron
> > from-the-north   and-bronze?

What shall we make of this? It is a question; the first word begins with a question particle (functioning in the Hebrew sentence a little the way the inverted question mark functions at the beginning of a written question in the Spanish language). "Iron from the north" is clear; it is one more reference to the military might of the foe from the north. Iron was used for weaponry, and whoever cornered the supply of iron would have immense supplies of weapons (compare 1 Samuel 13:19-22). (Perhaps that is part of the meaning of the imagery of the iron yoke about which Jeremiah spoke to Hananiah [28:13-14]; see our discussion in chapter VI.) The other two nouns in the verse should be taken together—"iron and bronze"; pairs like this were often split up into the parallel lines of poetry. The rebellious people had been called "bronze and iron" in 6:28, when Jeremiah was turning in his report to God on the "final examination." The noteworthy thing here in 15:12 is that there is a deliberate ambiguity as to which noun phrase is subject and which noun phrase is object: both "iron from the north" and "iron and bronze" can be either one. If we may paraphrase the verse, then, it seems to mean: Who will break whom? Will iron-and-bronze break iron-from-the-north, or the reverse? That is to say, God is telling Jeremiah to turn his attention from his local troubles with his local enemies to the larger conflict ahead, when the "brassbound" stubbornness of the people meets the "iron-and-steel" military might of Babylonia. It turns out, then, by this analysis, that God's answer in 15:11-12 is rather similar to his answer in 12:5-6.

Once more we have a "confession" and an answer, in 15:15-18, and 19-21, and this time the text offers plainer sailing for us. Our work on 2:2 (the word "remember," discussed in chapter III) and on 11:18-23 (the word "vengeance," earlier in this chapter) will help us with 15:15; the verse means, in effect, O Lord, thou art surely aware: take active notice of me, square accounts with me, obtain satisfaction for my sake from my persecutors. Do not lie down on the job: it is for thy sake that I am suffering rebuffs. This line of thinking is familiar to us by now.

Verse 16 we dealt with in chapter II in connection with our study of a chronology of Jeremiah's life: we suggested that "thy words were found" was a reference to the finding of the Deuteronomic scroll in 621 B.C., and that Jeremiah subsequently accepted his call; and the verse then goes on to suggest that the call to serve as God's prophet became in Jeremiah's mind a marriage substitute (he was celibate, after all). And we touched on verse 17 in connection with Jeremiah's ostracism from his fellows (see chapter VI). Jeremiah had no opportunity for the normal satisfactions of social relations; he was isolated because he had a quite special, grim task from God to perform.

Verse 18 brings something alarming: Jeremiah sees no end to

the sickness with which he is afflicted; God should be his deliverer, but where is he? He seems like a dried-up stream bed, an erstwhile brook that cannot be depended upon. But: Jeremiah once proclaimed God's word to Israel that God was the fountain of living waters, in contrast to leaky cisterns that hold no water (2:13)! Is God to be proclaimed as the never-failing spring *for Israel*, but *for Jeremiah* is he to be nothing but an undependable watercourse that dries up when the sun gets hot? This is a horrifying thought.

And God's answer again is not quite what one would expect. The first verse (verse 19) depends upon a fourfold use of the old verb "(re)turn." If you return," says God to Jeremiah, "I will let you return, and you shall stand before me." To stand before God suggests his functioning before him: in 15:1 the same phrase, used of Moses and Samuel, suggests their function as intercessors to God for the people. The parallel in 15:19 comes a little later on: "you shall be as my mouth." And then "turning" again; we may paraphrase Jeremiah's wording here this way: They shall depend upon you, but you shall not depend upon them. God is saying, in effect, Jeremiah, you have been proclaiming my word again and again to the people, "return, return" (compare 3:12, 22). Now I must say the same thing to you, "return." You need to do a little repentance yourself. Since when does your ministry depend upon public opinion? *Vox populi* is not *vox Dei*; you must depend upon me, not upon them, and they are dependent upon you to hear the word from me. One man with me is a majority. . . . As always, an easy word to say, but a hard word to live by. And God goes on to assure Jeremiah that if he is truly attentive to God and not to public opinion, he can in truth be a strong bronze wall and can expect God's deliverance. It is surely a paradoxical business, this help from God in hard times, as Jeremiah has been learning.

The next confession is found in 17:5-8. I am not aware that any commentator elsewhere has recognized this passage to be a confession, but my recent studies indicate that it does indeed belong in the series; and knowing it to be in the series, we shall find our understanding of it sharpened. On first reading it appears to be another variation by Jeremiah of Psalm 1: the contrast between the man who trusts in man, who is like a shrub in the desert that produces nothing, and the man who trusts in the

Lord, who is like a tree planted by the water, bearing fruit. And so the commentators. But we must affirm now what we suggested before, that if Jeremiah has offered these two variations on the themes found in Psalm 1 in the course of his confessions (we recall 12:1-2), then almost inevitably Psalm 1 must be earlier instead of later than Jeremiah. And if the earlier parody of Psalm 1 was a "personal affirmation" of Jeremiah's, rather than an affirmation about things in general, then the present passage may be a "personal affirmation" as well.

And so it turns out to be. Cursed is the man who trusts in public opinion, says Jeremiah; this is his attempt to follow out the lines of God's word to him in 15:19. The man who trusts in public opinion needs water (compare 15:18), as everyone does, but he is like a shrub in the desert that sees no "good" come ("good" here perhaps implies "rain," as it does in Deuteronomy 28:12, where God's "treasury of good" is equivalent to rain); the shrub stays dry and useless. But the man who trusts in the Lord is another matter. Notice that in the imagery here he is not likened to a tree planted by the rivers of water, as in Psalm 1:3—the imagery here is not static, as it is in Psalm 1; he is likened here to a tree planted by the water *that is not anxious when heat and drought come* but continues to bear fruit even during a dry spell. This is a new note; there is nothing like this in Psalm 1. *Both* the shrub in the desert and the tree by the water *equally* experience dryness, but the shrub has no firm rootage, while the tree does, so the tree outlasts the drought and continues to produce. This is the difference. Jeremiah has been experiencing dryness (15:18) but becomes convinced in this genuine expression of repentance that if he trusts in God rather than in public opinion he will survive the dry period when God appears to be a deceitful brook. In short, 17:5-8 is Jeremiah's response to God's call to repentance in 15:19-21.

The next confession (17:9-10) is more an expression of puzzlement than anything else: "The heart is deceitful above all things, and desperately corrupt; who can understand it?" The word translated "deceitful" here is used in Isaiah 40:4 of "uneven ground" which is bumpy, and the word translated "desperately corrupt" is the same word that was translated "incurable" in 15:18. The whole phrase in Hebrew is thus considerably more compact than the *Revised Standard Version* has it; one might

99

render it as follows: "The heart is rougher than anything, and incurable; who understands it?" God's answer is a reassurance: "I the Lord search the mind and try the heart" (actually the Hebrew says "search the heart and try the kidneys"—compare the *King James Version*—but the expression comes to the same thing), a reinforcement of Jeremiah's description of God's scrutiny in 11:20 (the words there are literally "kidneys and heart"). If there is anything like a chronological or psychological sequence to this material, then, it would appear that Jeremiah's musings are not in a direction of growing security in God.

This is the last reply recorded from God; there are further "confessions," but recorded without any matching responses. The next such confession is 17:14-18. Here we are back to the note of wounds and pain again (as in 15:18); Jeremiah had said that his pain refused to be healed, and at this point he asks God to heal him (verse 14). Then he goes on to quote the scoffers who ask (no doubt sarcastically) for some evidence of God's action; this is precisely what Jeremiah himself has been asking for—some action from God toward the scoffers—and now the scoffers claim to want it too. Isaiah gave voice to the same problem long before (Isaiah 5:19): scoffers who want some evidence of God's action. In verse 16 Jeremiah suggests that he has taken no personal pleasure in the bad news he purveys; it is a simple matter of bearing God's message—there is no added sadism on Jeremiah's part. But all the bad news has redounded onto Jeremiah; so turn it back once more upon them, O Lord!

No answer.

We begin again in 18:18 with a quotation from the people, who are convinced that it is business-as-usual with the religious leadership; nothing will come to an end, and they determine to "smite him with the tongue" (the tongue is an arrow, recall [9:8], and the word has power). Jeremiah's response to this is recorded in verses 19-23. The scoffers will not "heed" any of Jeremiah's words, but Jeremiah asks God to "heed" him and his "plea" (literally his "cause," as in 11:20). And then, deepening the pondering of the good which he wished for his people, and the evil which he has spoken out to them and the evil with which they have answered him, he continues, pathetically, "Remember how I stood before thee to speak good for them, to turn away thy wrath from them" (verse 20). At that point he gives himself over

100

completely to curse forms—one is reminded of Psalm 109:1-19 (psalm material which does not seem to appear in the responsive readings of our current hymnals!). Ferocious Jeremiah's words may be, but one must see them in the light of the long years of working and watching and waiting, and of speaking God's words to a people who seemed hopelessly deaf, and of wondering all the while where God's help really is. How long, O God? Come to! "When the time for your anger comes deal with them" (verse 23, *The Jerusalem Bible*).

No answer.

And again a confession (20:7-12), with quite startling opening words: "O Lord, thou hast deceived me, and I was deceived." The verb "deceive" here really means "seduce"—it is found in a law regarding seduction in Exodus 22:16—O Lord, thou hast seduced me, and I was seduced. Jeremiah is saying, I had thought that our relationship was best likened to a marriage bond (15:16, by implication)—but no, I was fooled, enticed, tricked by you; you had your fling with me and then tossed me aside.

There is another resonance to "deceive" here, and that goes back to the old story, to which we have referred so many times already, of King Ahab, the prophet Micaiah, and the four hundred yea-saying prophets (1 Kings 22:1-38). The explanation, we recall, by which Micaiah explained how it was that the four hundred spokesmen for God say "yes," wrongly, is that God intended to "entice" Ahab (1 Kings 22:20)—and this is the same verb that appears here in 20:7. Micaiah had said "no," rightly, and the four hundred had said "yes," wrongly, because God wanted to "entice" the king. Jeremiah had been convinced that he was saying "no," rightly, like Micaiah, and that the prophets who were saying "yes" were prophets of the lie (23:26). But now, reluctantly, he becomes convinced otherwise; he is the one who has been enticed, seduced, deceived, not the yea-sayers. At this point God becomes not only like a deceitful brook, like waters that fail (15:18), because he has failed to sustain Jeremiah and come to his rescue; far more seriously, Jeremiah is now questioning the very validity of his call from God, feeling that it is a will-o'-the-wisp, a phantom call, having no more solidity than the word of the four hundred long ago, or their successors in Jeremiah's own day.

Previously Jeremiah had mentioned the "merrymakers"

101

(15:17); now the joking and teasing is turned on him (20:7—"laughingstock" is a related word in Hebrew). He has been doing nothing but cry, "Violence and destruction!" (the same words appeared in 6:7), but all the mockers do is tease him about it.

The solution might seem obvious: quit! Simply withdraw from the obligation to speak out in the name of God. Merge with the population. But it does not work; the word is a fire (compare 5:14, 23:29) and he cannot keep it bottled up (verse 9). And people whisper constantly, "Let us denounce him!...Perhaps he will be deceived, then we can overcome him." It must be pointed out here that the verbs "deceive" and "prevail" have occurred several times in this passage, in different contexts. Jeremiah has accused God of "deceiving" him (verse 7); now the mockers look to the time when he will be deceived (verse 10). What they are planning to do, God has already done, according to Jeremiah; we have seen this ironic situation earlier, in 11:19, when his enemies wanted to kill him so that his name would be remembered no more, while God had already accomplished the matter by implication by the call to celibacy. Again, God has "prevailed" (verse7); the mockers want to prevail over him or "overcome him" (verse 10—it is the same verb in Hebrew). Again Jeremiah tries to hold in the words of God, but he says, "I cannot" (verse 9)—literally, "I do not prevail" (again, the same verb). Jeremiah is in a hall of mirrors: God should not deceive, but has; the mockers want him to be deceived, but he already has been; God should not overcome his own prophet, but has; Jeremiah wants to overcome the word, but cannot; the mockers want to overcome him, but need not try. Nothing is right, all is a-jangle.

The phrase in verse 10 translated "all my familiar friends" means literally "every person of my peace." "Peace" in Hebrew (_shālōm_) has to do with welfare and well-being. "Every person of my peace," then, is a precise equivalent of our current phrase "my support system"—and we sense once more how prostrated Jeremiah must have been when the support of his fellow villagers and of his kinsmen was denied him.

Jeremiah's only resort now is to a kind of rock-bottom affirmation of faith. In the old phrasing of the psalms, God was called "strong and mighty...mighty in battle (Ps. 24:8)." And on another occasion Jeremiah had used the word "ruthless" to

102

apply to his enemies (15:21), being assured that God would rescue him from them. Now, here in 20:11, Jeremiah brings these words together to describe God: he is the mighty, ruthless one, and again, he is convinced that his enemies will not "overcome" him, whether God ever overcomes him or not. And in verse 12 we have an exact repetition of 11:20; is this deliberately to reaffirm once more what he has affirmed earlier? Does he feel that a repetition of the old affirmation will reinforce his waning trust?

There was no answer to the two confessions in 17:14-18 and 18:18-23, and here, too, there is no answer—even though the words of 11:20 had brought forth an answer from God.

About verse 13, I confess I am baffled. It is a genuine word from Jeremiah; it has all the marks of his choice of vocabulary. Now it may be a quite sincere word uttered on another occasion but inserted here by a later editor as a fit conclusion to verse 12. Or, on the other hand, it may be in Jeremiah's mind a continuation of verse 12 on a note of affirmation in just the way that Psalm 22:24 follows directly on Psalm 22:20-21. Or again it might be ironic, hysterical, or sarcastic, considering the material which both precedes and follows it. There is no way I can see to decide the matter.

For verses 14-18 of this chapter plumb the depths of Jeremiah's bitterness and despair. The meaning of the passage is self-evident. We may note that in Israel to curse either God or one's parents was a capital offense (Leviticus 24:10-16, 20:9). Jeremiah teeters on the edge of the abyss, he does not quite take the plunge: he does not curse God, but curses the day he was born, which is to curse his call from God (1:5). He does not curse his mother but curses the day he was born, does not curse his father but curses the man who brought the news to his father of his birth. This is very near to madness and self-destruction, particularly for someone who has taken the enterprise with God so seriously as Jeremiah has. Rarely has the thought, "Why was I ever born?" been expressed so tellingly.

And of course there is no answer from God; it is hard to imagine how there could be.

We must back away, now, from the details of these outcries against God and speak first about the inheritors of this tradition of despair and suffering in Israel; second, about what might be

103

said by way of any response to the despair, and third about the whole curious business of this kind of dialogical struggle between a man and God.

First, the inheritors. The alert reader who is familiar with the Bible will see in this last confession a close resemblance to the book of Job. Indeed Job 3 is a long chapter which simply rings the changes on these five verses of Jeremiah. Since we have already noticed resemblances between Jeremiah 12:1 and Job, we are not surprised. Scholars are convinced that the great poem of the book of Job was written sometime after the time of Jeremiah.[5] It is quite likely that Jeremiah's words found real resonance among a people themselves prostrated by the dislocations of the fall of Jerusalem and consequent exile in Babylon, and that what Jeremiah had felt to be his special suffering, brought on by his acceptance of the office of prophet, other people likewise felt simply in the course of living out their lives in a time of widespread suffering. The poem of the book of Job therefore sets forth a good man—Everyman, if you will, not at all a special prophet but simply a good and righteous man—who suffers, it would seem, unduly, and who speaks out against God in a fashion pioneered by Jeremiah.

We have had occasion, also, to see a resemblance between Isaiah 53:6 and a phrase from one of the confessions (15:11). Now Isaiah 53:6 is part of the so-called "Suffering Servant" passage—that is, Isaiah 52:13—53:12. But there are more resemblances between Jeremiah's confessions and this "Suffering Servant" passage: Isaiah 53:7-8 offers phraseology very close to that of Jeremiah 11:18-19. In Isaiah 53 the prophet describes a servant who will live out a life of innocence, suffering for others, in order that the guilty may be restored to God's community. Isaiah 53 is part of the work of an anonymous prophet who lived toward the end of the time of the exile in Babylon; in this study, since we do not know his name, we shall simply refer to him as the "prophet of the exile." Scholars suggest a date for his work as approximately 540 B.C. It would seem plain that this prophet's vision of the suffering servant of God, like the poem of the book of Job, was deeply influenced by the experience and words of Jeremiah. There is a sense in which this whole perception of undeserved suffering as integral to God's activity is a kind of anticipation of the meaning of the crucifixion in the New

Testament (and it may well be that one reason that Isaiah 53 seems to describe the experience of Jesus in such an uncanny fashion is that Jesus himself not only knew the passage but took many cues from it as he lived out his ministry). So one might say that Jeremiah sensed that he was called to go the second mile for God; the poet of Job sensed that man's first mile of suffering should point beyond, to a validity past the normal range of rewards and punishments; and the "prophet of the exile" sensed that a servant must go the second mile for the world. Here is a point at which Christians will find a keen unity with the Old Testament.[6]

Now as to what our own response to Jeremiah's outbursts might be, it can, of course, take a variety of forms. Most people have moods—sometimes we're up, sometimes we're down—and so a tendency may be to say, take heart, Jeremiah, things may take a turn for the better. But this is of course not fair; down is down, and some people stay down, and perhaps some of us who constantly try to stay cheered up should be more realistically down. Honesty may demand it. The world may be a more fearful place than we realize. We may need to listen closely to the witness of Jeremiah, for our own answers may have been too easy.

And it will not do, either, to try to affirm that God is really nearest when he seems farthest away; again, this is to gloss over a very real situation with which Jeremiah is trying to grapple. Jesus is reported to have begun reciting the twenty-second Psalm as he was being crucified: "My God, my God, why hast thou forsaken me?" And whatever we do theologically with that cry of dereliction, no glib answer will do.

What we can do is what the Israelite community did, and what is perhaps the most surprising thing of all. They did not say, Mercy me, and then censor this material out of the logbook. They said, This, too, is part of the story; this, too, belongs in the testimony; this, too, we must teach to our children. And since they did listen and learn and absorb these cries of Jeremiah, more timid folk since then who have leaned in the direction of such thoughts have been emboldened to speak out, since Jeremiah had blazed the trail.

Now we have come a long way in our study of the prophet Jeremiah, and we have tended to lay aside a very basic question, which will have occurred to anyone who has paid attention to our explorations this far: How was it that Jeremiah perceived God to be speaking? And, in particular, what kind of mode of communication from God to the prophet can we imagine which would lead him into the kind of world view of dialogue, the he-said-and-then-I-said-and-then-he-said kind of situation?

We have spoken vaguely once or twice of trance states, but that is scarcely helpful. And as a matter of fact we have no ready knowledge of how Jeremiah became convinced of the reality of a voice which he accepted, which he felt constrained to share, which he felt to be like a fire in his bones if he did not. The verb in 1:4 which is translated "came"—"Now the word of the Lord came to me"—is perhaps not quite exact. It means something more like "happen"—"Now the word of the Lord happened to me." It was an event. Of the how's, we are not told. Presumably there was nothing photographable or tape-recordable about it. But it happened; and it was reinforced by a whole tradition in Israel, going back for centuries, as to how God dealt with his people.

And whatever else God was, he was conceived to be both personal and other. It was not a machine or a process that ran the world; it was a *personal* God. And Israel did not conceive her God to be merely a kind of sum total of the nationalistic ideals of the community (one could leave that notion to the devotees of the Baals!); God was quite *other* than Israel's own ideas about herself. This God who is both personal and other is a God of judgment and of grace. He tears, and he heals (Hosea 6:1). Given this dialogical quality to God's life with Israel (since *personality* and *otherness* imply dialogue), Jeremiah carried on God's side of the dialogue to the people, and then embarked upon his own dialogue with God when he could no longer make sense out of the events in his life. It was this three-way conversation which marks the book of Jeremiah as so special in biblical literature.

Now whether we ourselves, in our day, can gain any perspective for ourselves from this testimony of a three-way conversation from ancient times involving the deity, we will discuss in chapter X. But two other chapters must intervene. The first of these involves the matter of hope. We have heard of nothing so far but doom and destruction and death; is there no positive note, nothing to counterbalance the desolation? There is, though it takes some strange shapes. To this we now turn.

To Build
and to Plant

Before we examine the shape which visions of hope took for Jeremiah, we must attend to a preliminary question. There are indeed words of hope in the book of Jeremiah, notably in chapters 30 and 31, but the question to be faced is this: Are these words genuine to Jeremiah? Jeremiah himself insisted that "prophets...from ancient times prophesied war, famine, and pestilence against many countries and great kingdoms" (28:8); we would do well, then, to be cautious about words of hope which are attributed to Jeremiah.

And there is a special reason to be cautious. Much of the material in chapters 30 and 31 sounds very much like the phrases of the "prophet of the exile," that prophet responsible for Isaiah 53 (actually the compass of his poems is Isaiah 40-55). That prophet, we have said, lived about 540 B.C., a half century after Jeremiah. Compare these passages. First Jeremiah 30:10-11:

> Then fear not, O Jacob my servant, says the Lord,
>   nor be dismayed, O Israel;
> for lo, I will save you from afar,
>   and your offspring from the land of their captivity.
> Jacob shall return and have quiet and ease,
>   and none shall make him afraid.
> For I am with you to save you, says the Lord.

And this, from Isaiah 41:8, 10:

> But you, Israel, my servant,
>> Jacob, whom I have chosen,
>> the offspring of Abraham, my friend;
>
> •   •   •   •   •   •
>
> fear not, for I am with you,
>> be not dismayed, for I am your God;
> I will strengthen you, I will help you,
>> I will uphold you with my victorious right hand.

The resemblance is very close, so close that many commentators have doubted the genuineness of a good deal of the material in Jeremiah 30-31, feeling it to be a secondary reflection of the burst of hope given by the "prophet of the exile."

But we must beware of circular reasoning. It will not do to say, Jeremiah preached doom, so that any words of hope we see in the book of Jeremiah must be unauthentic. We could just as well reason in the other direction: If Jeremiah did preach hope, then what would his hope sound like? For it is plain that it is just as plausible to imagine that the "prophet of the exile" imitated Jeremiah when Jeremiah was in a hopeful mood as it is to imagine that some nameless follower of Jeremiah, a century or so after him, attributed to Jeremiah some words of hope which that follower had written in imitation of the "prophet of the exile." As a matter of fact, I have become convinced that this second way of reasoning is the correct solution; it is the "prophet of the exile" who imitated the diction of Jeremiah when Jeremiah was in a hopeful mood.

But first we must demonstrate to ourselves that Jeremiah did preach hope. And the first item to come to our attention is those last words of the call in 1:10, "to build and to plant." There is no way in which those words can conceivably be a later insertion into the call; they are built in to the structure of the poetry, as we saw in chapter II.

Two items in the record come next to our attention, items that concern the first deportation, the one in 597 B.C. in which King Jehoiachin and the queen mother were taken off to Babylon. In chapter 24 we read that after that deportation Jeremiah had a vision, much like the two visions recorded in 1:11-14: he saw two

108

baskets of figs on the altar—the first basket, of figs as good as first-ripe ones, and the second basket, of figs too bad to be eaten. And Jeremiah made the association between the folk in exile, who had been the "cream of the crop"—King Jehoiachin, who had hardly had a chance, and all the rest of the nobility—between those folk and the grade-A figs; and likewise between the folk who remained at home—King Zedekiah and all the rest—with the rotten figs. The folk in exile God will keep his eye on, and bring back, and use to "build" and "plant" again (verse 6); but the folk at home will be driven off and destroyed (verses 9-10).

Parallel with this vision is a letter Jeremiah wrote to those of the first deportation (chapter 29; at least verses 4-7 are genuine, and we shall confine our attention to these verses). He gave astonishing advice to them: Don't act like transients; don't just camp out. Settle down. "Build" houses and "plant" gardens. Plan marriages for your children; expand your families. And above all, pray to the Lord for the welfare of Babylon, for your welfare will depend upon her welfare. Now it is obvious to anyone that every prisoner of war in every prisoner-of-war camp dreams of release and nothing else, dreams of going home and nothing else. The idea of settling down where you are a prisoner of war, thinking of your future as *there*, to say nothing of praying for the welfare of your captors, is a stunning notion. And not just praying in a pietistic fashion for the individual soul of the local officer in charge, no; the word "welfare" in 29:7 is *shalōm*, "well-being, prosperity": the peace of Babylon, rather than her downfall! Jeremiah has here cast the people completely adrift from any dependence on a nation-state, on kingship, on an army, on borders, on Temple: without these, which most people assumed to be part of the given, part of the package deal of God's work with Israel, without these God has new, fresh work ahead for his people. But the action, for the time being, is in Babylon. Hope, yes, yet not hope along any familiar lines.

Then another gesture of hope, this time just before the final fall of Jerusalem in 587 B.C. Early in that year, when Jerusalem was under siege, Jeremiah got word from a cousin in his home village of Anathoth that he was needed to redeem a piece of family property that was in danger of falling to other ownership; the whole narrative is given in 32:1-15. (This incident may be the same as that referred to rather cryptically in 37:12, a passage we studied in chapter VI; we are not sure.) Was Jeremiah reconciled to his family by this affair? Or was there simply a rock-bottom loyalty which Jeremiah felt he must maintain with his family when it came to property matters, beyond any difference of opinion on religious matters? One wonders.

He slipped out of the city, then, and made his way to Anathoth and put up the money; we are told it was seventeen shekels, a little less than half a pound, of silver. We are given the picturesque details of the land purchase (32:10-14), but the main point of the incident—which, like many of Jeremiah's actions, served as a kind of acted parable—is to be found in verse 15, a word from God: "Houses and fields and vineyards shall again be bought in this land." It is almost as if I had inside news that the total financial structure of the United States was about to collapse (remember, we are within about a half year of the fall of Jerusalem, the end of everything), and even so I should go out and buy five hundred shares of A.T.&T., because "stocks and bonds shall again be traded in this land."

At several points, then, Jeremiah has affirmed his belief in "building" and "planting": in his vision of the good figs in Babylon, an image of the exiles who will come home some day for building and planting; in his letter to the exiles, urging them to build and plant in Babylon; and in his own purchase of property at Anathoth, as a gesture to the future, when houses and fields and vineyards will again be bought in the land. His understanding of "building" and "planting" was more than metaphorical.

Now that we have established that Jeremiah manifested a firm hope after all, we may turn to the material in chapters 30 and 31, where words of hope are concentrated—so much so that commentators have become accustomed to calling these two chapters "The Little Book of Hope."

The collection begins curiously, with a short oracle (30:5-7) which up to the last line does not sound like hope at all (and we shall speak of the last line in a moment):

> We have heard a cry of panic,
>   of terror, and no peace.
> Ask now, and see,
>   can a man bear a child?

110

> Why then do I see every man
>> with his hands on his loins like a woman in labor?
> Why has every face turned pale?
> Alas! that day is so great
>> there is none like it;
> it is a time of distress for Jacob.

Hardly hope here; nothing but war panic. And something rather special, which takes a bit of explanation. Traditionally one hurled at one's enemy various curses; indeed, we have already seen an array of these when Jeremiah asks God to deliver up the children of his enemies to famine, and all the rest (18:21-22), and there were many more traditional sorts of curses—may your wells become poisoned, may your cities become the lair of jackals, and so forth. And one of these, hurled at the enemy on the eve of battle, was, May your warriors become women. One finds this curse leveled at Babylon in Jeremiah 50:37. And such a curse has always been a persistent motif in the Near East; in the fall of 1970, when King Hussein of Jordan was reviewing his tank corps on the eve of his battles with the Palestinians, he noticed a brassiere tied to the radio antenna of one of his tanks. What is this, he asked? We have all become women, snapped the tank commander—that is, You have not yet unleashed us against the enemy.[1] Here in Jeremiah 30:6, however, it is the soldiers of Judah whom God is mocking for their acting like women. Why? Because God has declared war on his own people, so that it becomes fitting for him to throw the curse of warriors-become-women onto the soldiery of Judah.

No, there is no cheer here, nothing but darkest doom. And the last line, as I say, is curious; it reads, word by word in Hebrew, "and out of it he shall be saved," leaving us to ponder how these words could fit with what has come before. We must understand, of course, that the Hebrew text has no punctuation marks, no exclamation points or anything else; punctuation we must supply. Now I have two suggestions to make about this line. First, as it stands I think it has to be a sarcastic question, something like "and out of *this* he shall be *saved*??!!" Several considerations lead me to this conclusion. (1) The poetic parallelism demands a line of similar meaning to what has just preceded. (2) The verb "save" is never elsewhere used by Jeremiah for reassurance to the people (compare 2:27-28 and 8:20); this is not a conclusive argument, of course, but it is suggestive. (3) The word order of this line is unusual; in a Hebrew sentence the verb normally comes first. For something else to come first, especially a prepositional phrase, implies unusual emphasis—this is why I have translated it "and out of *this*. . ." with emphasis on "this." (4) If Jeremiah were announcing so drastic a switch in the situation as would be implied by a nonsarcastic, noninterrogative translation of the last line, he would probably not begin the line with "and." It is true, the word "and" in Hebrew sometimes means a mild "but" (for example, the "but" in the middle of 2:7 in the *Revised Standard Version* is "and" in Hebrew), but as strong a contrast as would be implied by an affirmation of rescue here would demand some stronger contrasting conjunction, and this we do not have. So I think the last line is intended, like the rest of the poem, to point to the hopelessness of Judah's military situation.

But—and this is my second suggestion about the line—the poem does come at the head of a collection of hopeful material, and as such was perceived to be a hopeful word by *someone*. I have always thought that someone else than Jeremiah misunderstood the passage and took it as hopeful, but now I am considering another possibility—that Jeremiah himself gave the oracle (which was an unchangeable word from God, after all) a new interpretation (sang it to a new tune?) and implied that the last line, after all, does mean "and out of *this* he shall be *saved*!!" There is some evidence elsewhere that prophetic oracles were occasionally given a "recap," so to speak, by having additional material added (we shall see an example in a moment in 30:12-17), so what we may have here is a doom oracle that has been given a fresh interpretation by Jeremiah himself at a time when he seems to have been released to speak of hope: perhaps verses 10-11 were added to verses 5-7 (verses 8 and 9 break the connection and were inserted later) as a reinforcement of this hopeful note. I feel certain, at any rate, that verses 10-11 are genuine to Jeremiah (in spite of my remarks at the beginning of this chapter); verse 11, in particular, contains many favorite phrases of his.

When we move to verses 12-15 we are back to a hopeless mood once more; verse 12 represents God speaking to the people in much the way Jeremiah had represented the people as speaking (10:19), indeed in much the way Jeremiah has spoken of himself

(15:18). Here is a perfect summary of the powerlessness of the Baals and of God's consequent declaration of war on the people (verse 14). Now the hopeless oracle that begins in verse 12 is finished in verse 15; we can be sure of this because of the presence here of a characteristic of this kind of poetry which very often appears, and that is that the end in some way imitates the beginning. Notice the sequence of words: in verse 12—"hurt," "incurable," "wound"; then in verse 14 fresh vocabulary— "lovers," "enemy"; then once more in verse 15—"hurt," "pain," "incurable." This is the sign of a rounding off; we are at the end. And what we have in these four verses is plainly the kind of doom-oracle with which we have become so familiar.

What comes in verse 16 is fresh: those who eat up Israel will in turn be eaten; the enemy will be destroyed. We must not be put off by the transitional word "therefore" at the beginning of verse 16 in the *Revised Standard Version*; the English word "therefore" certainly does not fit logically. The Hebrew word used here does often mean "therefore" but may imply a looser connection as well—"on this account"; or perhaps there is a small textual error in the Hebrew. In any event, we have here a sudden reversal in verse 16; and then in verse 17, where the description of the reversal continues, we have once more a reference to "wounds" and healing, an indication that we now have a *fresh* conclusion to the sequence that began in verse 12. Again, then, we seem to have a recap like that of verses 5-7 (and 10-11?); again what has seemed utterly dark has suddenly become light. Jeremiah offers no explanation as to how what is "incurable" (verses 12, 15) becomes curable (verse 17). Paradoxes never seem to bother the Old Testament prophets. God can veer off in new directions without warning; one is reminded of Jesus' remark, "With men it is impossible, but not with God; for all things are possible with God (Mark 10:27)."

Nevertheless it is helpful to raise the question as to what psychologically would trigger a fresh outlook in Jeremiah's perceptions; what would lead him from the darkest gloom to the kind of immoderate hope which we have seen? I think there is little doubt of the answer. What triggered it was the fall of Jerusalem. We have seen how Jeremiah recognized that the tradition of the prophets before him, who spoke in times of prosperity, was to speak of doom (28:8), and we have seen how

113

King Zedekiah hoped to hear from Jeremiah a fresh, new word from God (37:17). It was the task of the prophets to speak the word from God which could not be discerned from day-to-day appearances; in times of prosperity, they spoke darkly of doom, but conversely, when catastrophe had come, Jeremiah would perk up and begin to speak brightly of hope. The doom which he long foresaw had finally come, and he was released to begin to speak of building and of planting. We have already taken note of the way in which the first deportation from Jerusalem to Babylon stimulated him to words of hope to the deportees, and I have no doubt that the fall of Jerusalem likewise stimulated him to paint pictures of a bright future to those at home. The punishment had been administered; we can look to a new day ahead. And thus emboldened, Jeremiah added fresh and contrary additions to the old oracles of doom. So at least it would seem.

And another passage (verses 18-22) piles up the marvelous images of the time to come. It looks as if Jeremiah has here taken off from an old oracle of Balaam the prophet (Numbers 24:5-6), where the image of "tents" and "encampments" appears; and where the Balaam oracle itself goes on to speak of what God has "planted" (Numbers 24:6), Jeremiah goes on to speak of what will be "rebuilt" (30:18).

We have spoken of one source of Jeremiah's hopeful oracles, the recaps or additions to oracles of doom. But there is evidently another source to his hopeful oracles, and this source is illustrated by material in the first part of chapter 31. Let us look at the first oracle here, 31:2-6.

At first glance this passage seems like the other hopeful oracles. We notice here more reminiscences of old traditions—not to Balaam this time, but all the way back to the exodus from Egypt. We can read in Exodus 15:20 of the way Miriam "the prophetess" led the women of Israel with "timbrels" (a kind of tambourine) and dancing in celebration of the great victory over the Egyptians. The implication here in Jeremiah 31:4 is that there will be a new exodus; God's people will come back to the land again from their places of exile, just as God led them out of Egypt in the first place. And we notice once more the great themes of building and planting (verses 4-5).

But there is something new here—notice the proper names:

114

"Samaria," "Ephraim" (verses 5-6). Samaria had been the capital of the northern kingdom before it fell in 721 B.C. Ephraim was one of the northern tribes, whose territory was almost all that was left of the northern kingdom after the Assyrians had taken over much of it in 732 B.C., so that "Ephraim" became a convenient synonym for the northern kingdom. And what does Jeremiah say? That Samaria will be rebuilt and that Ephraim will come to Zion (the Temple area in Jerusalem) to worship God. What is involved here?

The point is that ever since the northern area and the southern area had split into two kingdoms after the death of Solomon, in 922 B.C., there had been dreams of reunion. Often this reunion was conceived of in a double way, both in terms of politics and in terms of worship: one ruling house and one central shrine. King Hezekiah seems to have made efforts in the direction of the reunification of north with south late in the eighth century (the situation is reflected in 2 Chronicles 30:1-17), King Josiah made similar efforts late in the seventh century (2 Chronicles 34:6-7), and the prophet Ezekiel was to dream of such reunion after Jeremiah's time (Ezekiel 37:15-23). What we evidently have here, then, is Jeremiah's word to the scattered *northern* tribes that they will come home some day; and of course such word need not have waited till the fall of Jerusalem—it could well have been proclaimed at any earlier time. All that Jeremiah needed to do was to go and stand facing the north, and speak; this is the situation assumed by 3:12a. (The action of facing north may not be historically accurate for the material in 3:12b-14a—we did not assume so when we dealt with the passage in chapter III—but it would be perfectly appropriate for a passage like 31:2-6.) And it need not bother us that no northerner was within earshot; the word, it was assumed, has power over an indefinite distance, as we have already learned.

The passage in question, then, 31:2-6, seems to have been an oracle originally directed to the north and then later incorporated into the growing collection of oracles of hope when the south needed reassurance too.[2]

Verses 7-9 of chapter 31 were similarly directed to the north (verse 9); so, quite likely, were verses 10-14, with the talk of "scattered Israel" and "Zion" (verses 10 and 12), although there

115

is no way to be sure. Verse 15, a poignant little verse, was evidently directed to the north; one of Rachel's children had been Joseph, the father of Ephraim (Genesis 30:24, 41:52). And obviously verses 16-20 fall into this category ("Ephraim," verses 18, 20).

What we have, then, for a good deal of 31:2-20 is another way in which the recap process was at work. Did Jeremiah himself take up oracles which he had originally destined for the north and reuse them for the south after the fall of Jerusalem? It is certainly more than possible.

Verses 21-22 could have been directed originally either to north or south, but this question is not the main problem with these two verses. The main problem is to understand their meaning and see how they fit into Jeremiah's overall thinking about hope. I have become convinced that these verses, and the oracle in 31:31-34 on the new covenant, are the twin capstones of Jeremiah's vision of hope, so let us pay close attention to them.

Before we examine the material in detail, however, let us remind ourselves of the basic situation after the collapse of Jerusalem. The issue, in Jeremiah's mind, would be twofold. The first was social-political—How could a scattered people be reconstituted and reunited?—and the second was theological—How could the punished people be restored to God? These two passages attempt to give the shape of an answer to these two questions.

The curious thing about verses 21-22 is that every word is understandable; it is the way the words fit together, and what the total meaning of the passage is, which causes difficulty. Verse 21 is clear; the exiles are to mark the way toward their place of exile with markers, cairns of stones or the like, so that they can find their way home again more easily—a kind of Hansel-and-Gretel procedure. The first half of verse 22 is fairly clear, also, though a couple of words in the *Revised Standard Version* may need to be put into a little better focus; John Bright's translation, "How long dillydally, O turnabout daughter?" perhaps catches it best. And the third line is plain, too: "For the Lord has created a new thing on the earth [or: in the land]." And what is this new thing?—"a woman protects a man." This was such a puzzle even in ancient times that early translations gave up and went in a variety of

116

directions, none of them very helpful. So Jerome, translating the Bible into Latin in the fourth century A.D., thought the line referred to the Virgin Mary's protecting embrace of the Christ child. But what can Jeremiah have had in mind here?

The word translated "protects" in the last line means "embraces"; it is found in the old poem in Deuteronomy 32:10, where it is said that the Lord found Israel in a desert land, and "encircled him," and "cared for him," and "kept him as the apple of his eye." In our Jeremiah verse the verb is plainly sexual; the Hebrew words suggest something like "the female embraces the he-man," and the term which I have rendered "he-man" is the same one found in 30:6, "Why then do I see every man with his hands on his loins like a woman in labor?" Is the reference in 31:22 similar to that in 30:6? It would seem so.

Actually there seem to be two slightly contrary images in Jeremiah's mind at this point. The first is a more expected image of femininity, that of innocence, vulnerability, endearingness. This is the way the prophets often addressed Israel or Zion: so "virgin Israel" here (verse 21), and the synonymous "daughter of my people" or "daughter of Zion" (for example, 4:11, 31), which mean something like "my darling people" or "darling Zion."[3] Israel off in the wilderness, then, is acting giddy, poor thing.

But the second image is the one found in 30:5-7, the warriors-become-women. Israel is not only acting feminine in the wilderness but effeminate. Stop it, says God, take heart; there is nothing I cannot do, and the next time around I will make the female rather than the male the initiator in sexual relations, so that the demoralized warriors-turned-to-women will no longer be under a curse. Next time women will take the lead.

Let us not misunderstand the situation. Our nerves are somewhat raw these days about the whole issue of the role of women in society, and we resent deeply the idea that warriors-turned-to-women is a curse; then, stumbling on this verse in Jeremiah, we may jump to the conclusion that we have an early anticipation of women's liberation. Both reactions are rather wide of the mark. We must insist that Jeremiah was a part of his time and took over the stock assumptions of his time (the curse of warriors-turned-to-women); he cannot be faulted for this. But there is really no archaic warrant here for women's liberation,

117

either, only an image tossed out as an indication both of the desperation of the people's plight and the marvelous innovativeness of God in dealing with it.

Make no mistake about it; the people *were* in a desperate situation. Assyria and Babylonia for hundreds of years had used the policy of deportation of populations as a means of control within their empires. The leadership of Samaria had been deported to the farther reaches of the Assyrian empire (2 Kings 17:6) and was never heard from again (archaeologists have recently dug up a pottery fragment from one of those regions with a handful of Israelite names inscribed on it; this is their only trace so far as we now know). [4] How can Humpty-Dumpty ever be put together again?

But nothing is too hard for God, and nothing is fixed in his program; only one thing in all the universe is fixed, and that is God himself. Do you feel paralyzed by the curse of effeminacy? Take heart; God can reverse even our sex roles, he can reverse the whole pattern set in motion in Genesis 3. Next time around the women will take the lead. In a way this little oracle is a theological companion to 4:23-26, in which likewise we saw a harking back to the creation narratives of Genesis 1-2. In that oracle, we recall, God felt the covenant people to be so much an experiment-gone-bad that creation might as well be torn up. Here the situation of the covenant people is so desperate that the only solution is a re-creation of creation. Why not?

But that Jeremiah should feel the need to reach back to Genesis to seek for warrant for a solution only underlines the desperation of the situation. And so we are left with this wild imagery—which was so wild, in fact, that it only puzzled later generations.

God has created a new thing on the earth in contemplating a reversal of sex roles; but another new thing he is doing: he will make a new covenant with Israel (31:31). (The only passages in Jeremiah in which the word "new" appears with any theological significance are these two.) And so we turn now to the "new covenant" passage, verses 31-34.

The first thing to say about the passage is that it seems to have a poetic form, though it is not so printed in the *Revised Standard Version*. (And we should note in passing that the phrase "and the house of Judah" in verse 31 should be omitted as a later addition to the text; Jeremiah is speaking to "Israel" in the sense of the whole people of God, not to the northern kingdom alone.) The first part of the oracle (up to "after those days, says the Lord," in verse 33) is framed in legalistic language, strange language for a poem—though even within the legalistic language one can find a structure; notice how the end of this section picks up the wording of the beginning. But then the last half, beginning with "I will put my law within them," breaks into a marvelous, soaring style, in great contrast to the legal phrases of the first part of the passage.

What is depicted here? The old contract is a dead letter; it is in the wastebasket, so God is going to draw up a new one which is different from the old one in crucial respects. One has the impression that the new one will not have the loopholes which the old one did. Is Jeremiah suggesting here that God has learned a thing or two from the first experiment, which failed? This is dangerous theological territory, but Jeremiah seems to have skirted it once before; in 2:5, we recall, God is depicted as asking whether there was any defect in his own conduct in the covenant (see chapter III). So here. What was the main loophole in the old contract? Well, its stipulations were written out on tablets of stone, The Ten Commandments, and posted for all to see. But the problem with posted rules is that people can obey them with their fingers crossed behind their backs, so to speak; they can obey them superficially or insincerely. (We recall "thou art near in their mouth and far from their heart"[12:2].)

The solution is that next time around God will put his law within people and write it on their hearts (verse 33)—the Hebrew word is singular ("heart"), not plural as various English translations have it. Now if the heart is the seat of the will and of plan-making, then this time people will obey God not because they are supposed to but because they want to. This time no fingers will be crossed behind one's back; this time "doing what comes naturally" will be doing what God wills. This is the miracle. As a result, the need for religious instruction will fade away: "No longer shall each man teach his neighbor and each his brother, saying, 'Know the Lord,' for they shall all know me, from the least of them to the greatest" (verse 34), from the smallest, humblest child to the oldest, most important citizen. There will no longer be a problem between God and his people, no barriers any longer (verse 34). God will be their God, and the people will be his people (verse 33).

If this passage were not so familiar to us, we would be as amazed by the wildness of the imagery which *it* contains as we are by the wildness of the imagery in verses 21-22. Both are wild; the idea that the old covenant from Sinai is a dead letter and is to be replaced by something as radical as the ingrafting of God's law into our internal organs was an unprecedented idea, and again demonstrates how serious Jeremiah understood the people's situation to be; the situation is far more radically wrong than most folk realize, he is saying. And the solution which he anticipates is almost like those recent experiments wherein scientists inject the amino acids representing the memory of the sound of a bell (amino acids derived from the bodies of rats previously trained to remember the bell) into the systems of mice so that they will thereafter recognize the bell without any training.[5]

God's solution to the social-political problem of a people scattered by exile is set forth in verses 21-22: God will make even the people's presumed effeminacy into a strength. And God's solution to the theological problem of a people rejected and destroyed by God is set forth in verses 31-34: God will draw up a new sort of contract for a new sort of relationship altogether, so that all the old difficulties will be gone and forgotten.

Now if Jeremiah's successors were puzzled by verses 21-22, they laid aside verses 31-34 as quite inappropriate. Indeed the "prophet of the exile" a half century later implied a strong dissent from the whole idea of a *new* covenant: "The word of our God will stand for ever (Isa. 40:8)." A promise is a promise. A contract is a contract. Once done, done forever. And this conviction of that later prophet became the prevailing conviction of subsequent Judaism. It is interesting; there are frequent instances in which early passages of scripture are quoted and dealt with once more in later passages of scripture—for example, the famous passages about swords into plowshares turns up both in Isaiah 2:2-4 and Micah 4:1-3, and then later on is even reversed (plowshares into swords) in Joel 3:10. But Jeremiah's vision of a new covenant is laid aside, never to be touched again in the Old Testament.

It waited a long time, until two dissenting groups of Jews

picked it up. The first group was the sect that produced the Dead Sea Scrolls; this group called itself the "members of the new covenant in the land of Damascus."[6] These sectarians, who had established their perfectionist community in the desert by the Dead Sea, were convinced that they were God's favored ones who had remained faithful to him, and that they were to wait and pray until God was to usher in his new age. They were convinced, in short, that God had bound himself specifically to them, that the passage in Jeremiah referred specifically to them; the rest of the Jews, they felt, belonged to the "children of darkness."

The other dissenting group of Jews were those led by that highly original theologian, Jesus of Nazareth. We are told that he stated, in the course of his last supper with his disciples, "This cup is the new covenant in my blood (1 Cor. 11:25)"; he evidently associated Moses' shedding of blood to ratify the covenant at Sinai (Exodus 24:8) with his own lifeblood about to be shed. And his followers picked up the cue and expanded on the idea in their writings, notably in the Epistle to the Hebrews, where the whole passage from Jeremiah is quoted and applied to Jesus (Hebrews 8:8-12; compare verses 6-7 there). The Christians, in short, were convinced that the passage in Jeremiah referred specifically to them; and of course the very phrases "Old Testament" and "New Testament" which we use mean "old covenant" and "new covenant."

One might object, of course, that Jeremiah's vision has not quite been achieved (compare 31:34), inasmuch as the process of religious instruction is still very much with us. But such an objection only dramatizes the innovativeness of Jeremiah's vision of hope; here, as in so much else, he was the most unconventional of prophets.

121

Chapter IX

Jeremiah Beyond Judah

We have acknowledged that Jeremiah's call was to speak hope as well as judgment, and now we must recall that Jeremiah's call was to a ministry with a scope far beyond Judah; he was appointed "a prophet to the nations" (1:5), and on the day of his acceptance of the call he was set "over nations and over kingdoms" (1:10). Up to this point in our study we have concentrated only on his ministry to Judah; now we must look at his ministry beyond the borders of the kingdom in which he lived.

Of a kind of "shadow ministry" to the lost northern kingdom of Israel we have already spoken in the previous chapter; we examined the oracles of chapter 31, which were evidently intended in the first instance to call home the exiles whose ancestors had been scattered out from Samaria more than a hundred years before, oracles then reused to give hope to Judah when she in turn faced a similar deportation. But we are more concerned now to have a look at his ministry to the nations outside the orbit of God's covenant. What of them?

Alongside the "Little Book of Hope," chapters 30-31, there is another subcollection of oracles within the book of Jeremiah, oracles against foreign nations (chapters 46-51). Here we find oracles against Egypt (chapter 46), the Philistines (chapter 47), Moab (chapter 48), other peoples east of the Jordan—the Ammonites, Edom, Damascus, Arab tribes farther east, and Elam off on the Persian plateau (chapter 49), and finally two long chapters of oracles against Babylon (chapters 50-51). That is to say, all these oracles depict a variety of disasters ahead for these various nations.

There is a double difficulty in examining these oracles. The first is that it was obviously much easier to fashion doom-oracles against other nations than doom-oracles against one's own; it was psychically cheaper, in other words—it took less effort and imagination to produce such oracles. It was true then, as it has been true since, that everyone considers other nations as peculiarly prone to wickedness, and subject thus to God's anger, and so the tradition of the production of such oracles was an old one in Israel, into which many prophets entered. When Jeremiah felt impelled, then, to speak out a doom-oracle against a foreign nation, he had a repertory of easy phrases for such a project which was not available to the same extent in the case of doom-oracles against his own people. One sees, for example, that the oracle against Moab is another version of material against Moab which is found in Isaiah chapters 15-16: compare, in particular, Jeremiah 48:29-38 with Isaiah 16:6-10 and 15:4-7, 2-3. The prophet Isaiah, as we know, lived a hundred years before Jeremiah did. The problem is, the material in Isaiah 15-16 is probably not authentic to the prophet Isaiah either (compare Isaiah 16:13!), but we cannot assign it a secure date.[1] Whatever the origin of the material, it entered into both the tradition of Isaiah and the tradition of Jeremiah. There was evidently occasion for such an oracle to be delivered in the course of Jeremiah's career (compare 27:3, an effort on the part of the Moabites and others to start a rebellion against Nebuchadnezzar), but whether Jeremiah delivered any or all of chapter 48 on this or some other occasion we cannot learn. Perhaps only a nucleus of this chapter is genuine to Jeremiah and part of the material written later; it is hard to say.

The other difficulty is parallel to this: later generations, anxious to attach Jeremiah's name to their own hatreds, seem to have been impelled to draft doom-oracles against foreign nations and then attribute them to Jeremiah. This may be the case with the oracle against Edom (49:7-22); verses 14-16 are almost word-for-word found in Obadiah 1-4, and since hatred of Edom seems to have been at its height in the years after the fall of Jerusalem (compare Lamentations 4:21-22), the book of Obadiah may well

123

have been written then and this portion of the poem attributed to Jeremiah also; but again we do not know.

The point is this: the constructing of oracles against foreign nations was both an easy and an attractive task, and some of what we find under Jeremiah's name in this collection may well be traditional and earlier than Jeremiah, and some of it may be later than Jeremiah and simply attributed to him: but in any case a good deal of it lacks the striking marks of Jeremiah's poetic style which we have found elsewhere.

One inevitable result of this whole situation is that it is more difficult for the modern reader to become engrossed in what Jeremiah or anyone else may have proclaimed about what God was about to do, say, with the Moabites. We have never met a Moabite personally, and the immediate fate of the Moabites in ancient times is remote from our interests. We become more involved in the question of what God intends to do with his own covenant people, since we find ourselves in that tradition; we sense that God might in some way be talking about us, seeing that the covenant bond has historically involved folk with whom we can identify.

Nevertheless, even with these difficulties, some of the material may be worth examining. Let us try.

We begin at the beginning: 46:3-12 is an oracle against Egypt at the time of the battle of Carchemish (605 B.C.). We recall (see chapter V) the circumstances of the battle; it was the high-water mark of Egyptian penetration into Asia against Babylon. Egypt was roundly defeated, and on the eve of that battle Jeremiah evidently offered this oracle. It is full of his touches: the phrase "terror on every side" in verse 5 (compare 20:1-6 and 20:10, and 6:25 as well), and the wording of verse 12, which recalls 6:21.

The second poem in this chapter (verses 14-24) is likewise genuine to Jeremiah—some pun on the name of the pharaoh of Egypt is implied in verse 17, though we can scarcely reconstruct it. One can read the passage aloud; all the strange names are unfamiliar in one's mouth, but one can well imagine the vividness of such lines to the original hearers for whom the names were the stuff of headlines. We cannot now identify the specific historical circumstances which gave rise to this poem, but we recognize that many people in Judah always hoped that Egypt would come to their rescue, and words which humiliate the Egyptians, which shatter their military reputation, must have struck terror in the ears of Jeremiah's peers who always had hopes from that quarter.

Chapter 47 is another vivid poem, no doubt authentic to Jeremiah. The Philistines, a traditional enemy to Israel (we recall their capture of the Ark of the Covenant when Shiloh was destroyed—see chapter V), were living along the coast west and south of Jerusalem. Nebuchadnezzar sacked the city of Ashkelon in 604 B.C., and it was evidently in response to this emergency that King Jehoiakim proclaimed a fast in Jerusalem, the occasion when Jeremiah's scroll was read to the king (36:9). Again, says Jeremiah, there is no holding back the Babylonians; Ashkelon will perish (verse 5).

In all these oracles Jeremiah is speaking out against nations with whose fate Judah is tied. Jeremiah does not speak out any oracles in a vacuum; there are never any "oracles in general." The oracles against foreign nations which we have been examining are spoken out in the context of events which are of high importance to Judah. Though Jeremiah understands them to be spoken directly by God to the nation in question, the inhabitants of Judah are very much the concerned bystanders!

Let us skip over chapters 48-49, which, as we have seen, consist in large part of anonymous material, and turn to the enormous collection of oracles against Babylon in chapters 50-51. One can imagine why the collection is so big. Babylon was *the* issue of those days. Jeremiah could speak all he pleased about the inevitability of the fall of Jerusalem to Babylon, could speak all he pleased about the necessity of the Jewish exiles in Babylon to settle down and to pray for their captors, but if Jeremiah was to speak any word of hope, of restoration, of the return of the exiles to build and to plant, then the ultimate question of the fall of Babylon needed to be faced. How? When?

We may begin at the end, with a symbolic act of Jeremiah's (51:59-64). We know of no such delegation to Babylon otherwise, but there is no reason to doubt the story. Indeed, it is all quite natural. Seraiah the quartermaster, to whom Jeremiah turned, was the brother of Baruch the scribe (both were sons of Neriah, the son of Mahseiah; compare 32:12 and 36:4). Plainly Jeremiah had open access to him. And while Jeremiah might well believe in the efficacy of the word of God against Babylon over a distance of five hundred miles, there would certainly be no harm in giving strong reinforcement to the word by entrusting a written copy of the message against Babylon to the delegation as it leaves, and then having its members reinforce it still more by sinking the book to the bottom of the Euphrates river to symbolize the sinking of Babylon.

For God of course is not permanently pro-Babylonian; Babylon is only an instrument in God's hands. Compare the extraordinary poem in 51:20-23 (whether from Jeremiah's mouth or not), on Babylon as the hammer that smashes everything in sight, and note that that instrument, when it has served its purpose, will in turn be smashed (50:23). But in all this array of poems we cannot be sure what is from Jeremiah and what is not. For example, the word in 6:22-24, regarding the foe from the north which is to destroy Zion, is now given, almost word for word, as a word against Babylon (50:41-43). Is this irony on Jeremiah's part? Or is it simply the work of a later imitator (perhaps excited by the actual coming of Cyrus of Persia, marching down on Babylon from the north, just before 538 B.C.)? There is no way to be certain.

And in a way it does not matter anyway. We have tried very hard during our study of Jeremiah to discern the man and his own message, to visualize the prophet. But this is not what primarily interested his community. To his community these words were words from God, and when further words, likewise conceived as words from God, became attached to the tradition of a prophet, the collection was all the richer. Our own concern for copyrights was no concern in Jeremiah's community. And we must be content with less than certainty when it comes to these words against foreign nations, for these are words in which everyone wanted to have a hand.

Toward the end of chapter V we made reference to Jeremiah's final days, in Egypt with Baruch. Since the closing events of his career do seem to have taken place outside Judah, it is appropriate here to trace these events in more detail.

We pick up the story at the time of the final fall of Jerusalem in 587 B.C. (see chapter VI), when Zedekiah escaped the city, was captured, blinded, and sent to Babylon to die.

The Babylonians then turned to the descendant of an old noble

126

family and appointed him governor of the Babylonian province of Judah: Gedaliah, the son of Ahikam, the son of Shaphan (39:14, 40:5). Members of this family have been in and out of our story the whole time, but we have not really sorted them out. They are as follows:

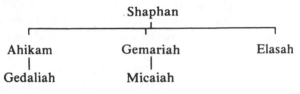

The grandfather, Shaphan, had been secretary and financial officer to King Josiah and had carried the newly found Deuteronomic scroll to the king (2 Kings 22:3-13), and his son Ahikam was part of the delegation which was sent by the king to a prophetess to verify the authenticity of that scroll (2 Kings 22:12-14). Then when Jeremiah preached the Temple Sermon and was in danger of being condemned to death, it was Ahikam who protected him (26:24). When Jeremiah's own scroll was read by Baruch in the Temple, it was the grandson Micaiah who brought the news to the court of King Jehoiakim (36:11), and his father, Gemariah, present at court (36:12), was among those urging the king not to destroy the scroll (36:25). When, soon after the first deportation in 598 B.C., King Zedekiah sent a delegation to Babylon, a third son, Elasah, was in the delegation, which, along with its other tasks, carried a letter to the exiles from Jeremiah (29:3). The whole family was, in short, a family of prestige with whom Jeremiah had been very much involved during his whole career.

Thus it was Gedaliah whom Nebuchadnezzar appointed to be governor of the newly organized province of Judah, and as soon as the military occupation began, Jeremiah was recognized by the Babylonian authorities as a "friend" (39:11-12). One can imagine that Jeremiah might have been just as uncomfortable over the Babylonian assumptions of his loyalty to them as he had been earlier when the Jewish military authorities had accused him of going over to the enemy (37:13); it would not have been any easier to explain his theological position to the Babylonians. Jeremiah, then, was released from the guardhouse into the custody of the

127

newly appointed governor, Gedaliah (39:13-14). But Jeremiah had remembered while still in the guardhouse to give a word of encouragement to Ebed-melech, the Ethiopian official who had rescued him from the muddy cistern (39:15-18).

Gedaliah's administration was set up not in Jerusalem, which at this point was evidently uninhabitable (compare Lamentations 2:13, 4:1), but in Mizpah, a few miles to the north. There was guerrilla resistance to the Babylonian occupation continuing in the countryside under the leadership of a man named Ishmael, who was of royal stock (41:1), as Gedaliah evidently was not. When one faction makes peace with a military occupation, no matter how "sensible" that policy might seem (compare 40:10), there will inevitably be another faction claiming legitimacy and carrying on the struggle in the name of patriotism.

Ishmael was plotting to assassinate Gedaliah, and although one of the guerrilla leaders, a man named Johanan, tried to warn Gedaliah of the plot, the latter did not take the warning seriously (40:13-14). Ishmael then carried out his plan and assassinated the governor (41:1-3); we are not told how long Gedaliah had served in that capacity. After the assassination, Ishmael ambushed a party of pilgrims from the north (we are not told what his motives were) and killed all but ten, who were able to buy their lives, but they remained captives of Ishmael (41:4-10). Johanan, the one who had tried to warn Gedaliah beforehand, took off after Ishmael; when he overtook him, he was able to rescue the captives, but Ishmael escaped to the other side of the Jordan, to the Ammonites, who were sponsoring and protecting him (41:11-18; compare 40:14).

This group of captives was uncertain what to do; if they remained in the country, they could be suspected by the Babylonians of being anti-Babylonian (Ishmael had spared their lives, after all), while if they fled they would be suspected of guilt. Johanan was asked to press Jeremiah for some guidance from God as to what they should do: Jeremiah, receiving word from God, told them to stay in Judah, but evidently there was dissention in the camp and the group determined to slip away to Egypt, out of harm's way (chapter 42); they somehow became convinced that Baruch was unduly pressuring Jeremiah (43:1-3). All this tugging and hauling suggests the emotion and confusion of people torn by events and unable to reach any decisions.

128

They joined a larger group of refugees and went off to Egypt, taking Jeremiah and Baruch with them, not as hostages so much, perhaps, as an available source for a word from God (43:4-7). One can imagine how unwillingly Jeremiah went along.

He evidently continued to be convinced of the power of Babylon, for no sooner had the group arrived at Tahpanhes, on the edge of the Nile Delta, than Jeremiah set forth another "acted parable": he set stones in the pavement in front of Pharaoh's palace, insisted that Nebuchadnezzar would set up his throne there, and said that in general Babylon would sweep the land of Egypt as clean as a shepherd does who delouses his cloak—not a very elegant view of the power of Egypt! (43:8-13).

The last chapter in the narrative of Jeremiah which we find in the book is chapter 44, and we need to spend a bit of time with it because it faces us with one of the most basic issues for the Old Testament: How is one to interpret the events of history?

Jeremiah confronts people who have been continuing the practice of worshiping Astarte, the fertility goddess, and speaks in the name of God: Why do you not take a lesson from history? Can you not understand that it was I who destroyed Jerusalem because of all your disobedience and disloyalty in burning incense to other gods? And why do you continue to do so in Egypt? Will you never learn? I will punish you here as I punished you in Judah; none of you will survive to go home to Judah (44:1-14).

Then the devotees of Astarte confront Jeremiah and say, in effect, When we worshiped Astarte during Manasseh's reign, we prospered. When we left off worshiping her at the time of the reign of King Josiah and went back to the worship of Yahweh, what happened? Disaster. Josiah was killed in mid-career, and Jerusalem fell, all because we abandoned Astarte (44:15-19).

Jeremiah repeats the word and says, as he said once to Hananiah, All right, wait and see whose word will stand, mine or theirs (44:28).

We saw, at the very beginning of our study, how two prophets could differ in their interpretation of the distant past, two prophets as validated as Jeremiah and Ezekiel (see the beginning of chapter III). Now we see that the events of the immediate past can likewise be open to a variety of interpretations; both Jeremiah the Yahwist and the folk devoted to Astarte can find validation in the events of the preceding century for their own ideology. Events

129

do not bring with them an inevitable interpretation; events are to some extent, at least, ambiguous. It is the spokesman for a particular theology who brings to the same events his own interpretation, which then seems self-evident to him. It is never easy to be sure, at the time, which is right; one must commit oneself to a theology, a world view, and then let that mode of interpretation do its work on events as they unfold. It is a sobering thought to those of us who had assumed that for folk in those days all was clear. It was not.

This is the last we hear of Jeremiah, still haranguing the refugee camp in the name of Yahweh. It is curious: we have no clues as to how either Jeremiah or Baruch ended his days. As for Baruch, we do not even have any clues as to how he began to pull together the material which eventually became our book of Jeremiah. We wonder, Did Baruch himself stay in Egypt and die there? Did his brother Seraiah stay in Babylon, or was he included in the second or third deportation to Babylon (52:29-30)? Did Baruch send a copy of his record of Jeremiah's words and deeds to Seraiah? All this is guesswork. But it is even more noteworthy that we have no notice of how Jeremiah's own life ended. It is strange. The ancients looked for happy endings to their narratives even more insistently than we do, and if there had been any kind of satisfactory ending to the story of Jeremiah which Baruch had known—how he died, where he was buried— we must assume that Baruch would have recorded it for us; on the contrary, if Jeremiah had been martyred—stoned to death, for example, as a late legend imagined that he was[2]—then Baruch would have seen that event (if he had learned of it) as part and parcel of a life lived out in suffering obedience to God, and one might imagine that this narrative, as well, would have been recorded. As it is, we have nothing.

Still, it is worth our while to speculate for a moment how it is that we have as full a knowledge as we do of Jeremiah's career, far fuller than for any other prophet. Why would Baruch have taken the trouble to record as much as he did?

Perhaps the answer lies in that threat of his fellow villagers so many years before: "Let us cut him off from the land of the living, that his name be remembered no more" (11:19). That was the constant threat, made far more real, as we have already seen, by God's call to Jeremiah to abstain from marriage and family.

130

Having no sons to carry on his name, facing utter chaos in Judah, waylaid into a refugee camp in Egypt, Jeremiah faced the real possibility that his name would be remembered no more. When Jeremiah could not be in the Temple area personally, he had a scroll sent instead. An enlarged scroll, then, with written memory of the man's life, might have to be the substitute for sons, so that his name would be remembered after all. And so Baruch evidently undertook the task, in an effort to keep his name alive.

Many years later, in another context, another prophet would say, regarding men who had been mutilated and were unable to father a family, "I will give in my house and within my walls a monument and a name better than sons and daughters; I will give them an everlasting name which shall not be cut off (Isa. 56:5)." It seems to have been so with Jeremiah.[3]

Chapter X

Spokesman Out of Time

We face two tasks as we sum up what Jeremiah may mean to us. The first is to assess how he fits into the whole tradition of which we are the heirs, and the second is to ask whether God speaks to us now through the story of Jeremiah and, if so, how. This second task will take up the major share of this chapter, but first things first; let us round out our historical understanding of Jeremiah by seeing how he fits into the total biblical tradition.

Jeremiah stands very closely related both to those who came before him and to those who came after him. It is plain from our study that he was indebted to predecessors in his prophetic tradition: he drew from Elijah, from Amos, from Hosea and Micah and Isaiah. But he was equally indebted to others, besides prophets, who came before him: to Moses and the tradition which had grown up about Moses, to psalmists, to the circle of tradition which gave rise to the book of Deuteronomy. But if he was indebted to those who came before him, he equally contributed to those who came after him. We have taken note (at the end of chapter VII) how both the poet of the book of Job and the "prophet of the exile" who produced Isaiah 40-55 were in debt to him: the one in framing a dialogue of struggle with God and an exploration of how it is that an innocent man can suffer; the other in the vocation for suffering which that anonymous prophet saw to be crucial in God's purpose. But we could equally trace Jeremiah's mark on his immediate successor, Ezekiel, on the little book of Jonah, and on other material which emerged in the course of centuries in the Old Testament tradition. In many and various ways the Jewish community was nourished by his words and his story.

By the same token, the New Testament tradition is greatly indebted to Jeremiah. Jesus himself carried on and deepened the prophetic tradition in the direction in which Jeremiah set it (insofar as we can discern Jesus' own message and sensibilities). We have seen how Jesus picked up from Jeremiah's Temple Sermon the "den of robbers" phrase (7:11) when Jesus turned the money changers out of the Temple, and we have noticed also the way in which his cry of dereliction on the cross echoes so directly Jeremiah's expressions of abandonment by God (see once more chapter VII). But many sayings of Jesus seem to be echoes of Jeremiah; for example, Matthew 11:29, "Take my yoke upon you, and learn from me; for I am gentle and lowly in heart, and you will find rest for your souls," where the last line is surely modeled on a line in Jeremiah 6:16. And, more profoundly, in his own lifetime Jeremiah was an explorer of the way of the cross. We may have the impression that Jeremiah was a less willing explorer of this way, and that Jesus (so far as the tradition goes) a more willing one, but even so we must reckon with Jesus' cry in the garden of Gethsemane, "Remove this cup from me (Mark 14:36)." In any event, it remains true that Jeremiah was an explorer in the same direction. The tradition which Matthew reports, that some folk thought that Jesus was Jeremiah come to life again (Matthew 16:14), reflects in a shorthand way an acute awareness of this resemblance.

(And in passing we may suggest that if we ever have occasion to wonder about the nature of Jesus' own inner life, his own self-understanding, then we might well find indirect but suggestive resources in the story of Jeremiah, who anticipated him in so many ways. Jesus evidently included "prophet" among the categories which he applied to himself [we note Mark 6:4 and Luke 13:32-35], and the insight which we gain into the inner life of Jeremiah may give resonance to our understanding of Jesus.)

Paul likewise reflected more than once on the material of Jeremiah: one thinks, for example, of Galatians 1:15, "But when he who had set me apart before I was born, and had called me through his grace," and its resemblance to the opening words of Jeremiah's call in Jeremiah 1:5. We have seen (chapter VIII) how

133

the Epistle to the Hebrews takes over the whole of the "new covenant" passage and makes Christian testimony out of it. And the book of Revelation is crowded with reminiscences of the book of Jeremiah: the "springs of living water (Rev. 7:17)," to cite just one passage, is plainly a reflection of Jeremiah 2:13.

Thus it was not only that the book of Jeremiah itself became scripture for later generations but also that the words of that book themselves gave rise to many fresh expressions in the words of men of later generations, words which then in their turn became scripture. Thus even though Jeremiah may have thought of himself as socially isolated in his own lifetime ("I sat alone," 15:17), in the long run he emerges as part of a consistent company which spans many centuries of the biblical tradition.

Let us turn to the second task in our summing up, and ask whether God speaks to us now through the story of Jeremiah and, if so, how. This is a new kind of question with which we have not yet grappled. The attentive reader will have noticed that up to this point in our study we have avoided making statements like "God speaks to us now through Jeremiah"; instead, we have confined ourselves to statements like *Jeremiah was convinced that God spoke through him to his people.* This latter kind of statement may have seemed cumbersome to some readers, but it was used deliberately.

That is to say, up to this point in our study we have looked at Jeremiah as we might look at any other figure whose life and teachings have had an impact on the world—as one might look at Socrates, say, or Lincoln or Gandhi. We have attempted to become well enough acquainted with the story so that we become involved in it and can react positively to it. We have learned to appreciate a fellow human being, to enhance our view of the possibilities of humankind, to enlarge our perspective on what is best and finest from our past.

But of course a general humanistic approach is not all that the material seems to demand. On the face of it, Jeremiah came before his peers not as a thoughtful teacher from whom people could learn something but rather as a spokesman for Almighty God, and though a good many people evidently dismissed his claim or ignored it, other people just as obviously took his claim seriously and took his messengership to heart, particularly in the years that followed the tragedy of the fall of Jerusalem. And in the centuries that followed, the collected material about Jeremiah, together with similar material from other prophets, would begin to be laid alongside Deuteronomy and the other books of law and history which were being looked upon in the Jewish community as authoritative, as scripture; and then the Christian church, which grew out of the Jewish community, took over that body of scripture and continued to maintain the conviction that this was scripture for the church as well.

So the kind of statement we have been making so far—"Jeremiah was convinced that God spoke through him to his people"—is not enough. That kind of statement is a statement about one man's belief in the past; it is a historical statement, a verifiable statement (at least theoretically so). We must begin instead to see whether the second kind of statement—"God speaks to us now through Jeremiah"—is a meaningful way to speak. That kind of statement is a theological statement, a statement of faith on our part; a statement of faith that God exists, that a man named Jeremiah heard God rightly, or at least rightly enough to be helpful to his peers and to later generations in their listening to God, and that we ourselves can hear God rightly enough through the material of Jeremiah to be able truly to respond to God. This kind of statement is of course not verifiable in the same kind of way as the historical statement could be. "Faith is the assurance of things *hoped for*, the conviction of things *not seen* (Heb. 11:1, italics added)." The question of whether the kind of statement which is a statement of faith is a useful way to talk is a far more complex problem than most of us have recognized.

Plainly Jeremiah was a part of a very particular and unique historical situation. In his time the fall of Jerusalem loomed, and then it happened. A specific government had been in specific difficulties and then disappeared. These circumstances prevailed once and will never recur. In what way, then, do later generations have any justification for lifting Jeremiah's story out of its original matrix and making it their own, for their own particular and unique times? One of my colleagues puts the issue this way: "All scripture is a pilgrim, wandering through history, engaging in new settings, and ever refusing to be locked in the box of the past."[1] Jeremiah himself, so far as the evidence goes, had no eye

135

for the far future, for our future. His eye for his near future was to a future in the hand of God which grew directly out of the choices which his own people were making as he spoke. How are we justified, then, in casting Jeremiah adrift from his mooring in the seventh and sixth centuries B.C. and allowing him to lodge in our present? If we do this, is he still recognizably Jeremiah? And in this process, can we hear God? And, if so, how?

There are a number of wrong ways to answer such questions. For example, when we first hear the material from the prophets, when we hear their passion for justice and their appeal for repentance, we are often deeply moved and want to apply such words directly in our own situation. Thus if Jeremiah addressed King Jehoiakim as to how he should be sensitive to the will of God, we may jump to the conclusion that the head of government of the nation to which we belong—a president of the United States, for example—stands under analogous judgment from God, and that God's words through Jeremiah to King Jehoiakim are directly applicable to our own nation. But there are some false steps here. The United States of America is not directly comparable to the kingdom of Judah in the Old Testament, not only in the political sense that Judah was a small state threatened by large imperial powers, while the United States is not a weak nation in the same way, but even more profoundly in the theological sense. That is, the kingdom of Judah understood herself to be a part of the people of God called Israel, called by God to be his blessed community in the world, a demonstration to the world of what community should be; and she understood herself thereby to stand under both the special judgment and the special grace of God. Two verses from the book of Amos put it neatly: "Hear this word that the Lord has spoken against you, O people of Israel, against the whole family which I brought up out of the land of Egypt: 'You only have I known of all the families of the earth; therefore I will punish you for all your iniquities (Amos 3:1-2).' " But this is not the self-understanding of the United States of America, or of Canada or Great Britain or any other modern state. We reserve to another category altogether our understanding of membership in the "people of God"; we think of membership in the Jewish community, in the Christian community, perhaps in other communities, but we do not think (or at least we should not) that God's blessings and God's will are

136

concentrated today on any single *nation-state*. Therefore the words to the king of Judah, no matter how pungent and moving, are not directly applicable to any national leaders today. Put it another way: if the United States of America has sinned (and it has, of course—as all persons and political groups have sinned), one still cannot realistically expect a president of the United States to affirm this and, speaking for the American people, to repent and contritely ask forgiveness of God. One might hope for an expression of regret on the part of a president for wrongdoing committed by the American people, but not for repentance *on behalf of the American people.* This is not his job. It is the calling of various religious leaders on behalf of their respective communities, and indeed on behalf of all of us, but not the task of a national president. This is not the task for which he is elected. His primary mandate is not head-of-the-people-of-God but rather elected-executive-under-the-Constitution. And the Constitution is a human document voluntarily accepted to a reasonable degree by all its citizens, whether they acknowledge God or not.

In short, our understanding today about how God works, and through which groups and people he works directly, and through which groups and people he works indirectly, is so different, and colored (for Christians at least) so much by the intervening material of the New Testament, that though we may have a keen feeling that Jeremiah's words from God are applicable, we may not be able to say very directly *how* they are applicable. And the specific crucial problem is raised by that intervening material of the New Testament. Do we understand the Old Testament message to be *replaced* by the New Testament message? Or *supplemented* by the New Testament message? Or *explained* by the New Testament message? If the Old Testament message is replaced by the message of the New, then the Old Testament message is really irrelevant except as a kind of curious and defective preliminary trial run—and that would include the material from Jeremiah. On the other hand, if it is explained by the New, how are the contrasts between the Testaments to be understood?

We are in a tangle of issues here. So let us back away and resort to a couple of related parables to see if we can gain some clarity. The first parable is suggested by a remark of Oscar Cullmann many years ago in his suggestive book *Christ and Time:* "The

137

decisive battle in a war may already have occurred in a relatively early stage of the war, and yet the war still continues. Although the decisive effect of that battle is perhaps not recognized by all, it nevertheless already means victory. But the war must still be carried on for an undefined time, until 'Victory Day.'"[2] He is suggesting by this illustration the situation of the Christian, whether of the mid-first century or the twentieth, who is living "between the times": the decisive battle (Christ over Satan) has already occurred, though the victory (God's kingship) is not yet apparent to everyone.

Let us extend his illustration slightly. Let us imagine a crowd gathered underneath the balcony of the royal palace in a kingdom, and a spokesman suddenly appearing on the balcony. He has great news, he says; the cruel old king has been dethroned and imprisoned, and revolutionaries are about to declare a republic. And in this civil war the spokesman appeals to the crowd for support, food, arms, so that the struggle may continue and be crowned with success. A choice is now before each man, woman, child in the crowd: Shall we trust the self-proclaimed spokesman on the balcony or not? Is he telling the truth? Or is he perhaps a madman? Or (terrible possibility) is he an *agent provocateur* of the cunning old king, a king still thoroughly in control, who seeks by this trick to entrap some of his subjects into declaring themselves against him, so that he may rid himself of any opposition? This, we might suggest, is the choice we face as we listen to the appeal of the New Testament to its call to decision. Remember, we cannot *prove* the validity of the news from the spokesman on the balcony: "Faith is the assurance of things hoped for, the conviction of things not seen."

But our situation with an Old Testament spokesman is still more complex, and we may illustrate this by a further extension of our parable. Imagine, some years before the scene on the balcony which we have just portrayed, another scene. The king, we remind ourselves, is cruel in his kingdom, and some of his subjects have begun to wonder whether they will ever be delivered from his rule. A day comes when one of the king's subjects idly turns the knob of his shortwave radio receiver. He accidentally picks up a broadcast from a neighboring state. Now that neighboring state has no cruel king but instead, something perhaps even worse, a military dictatorship ruling by a secret police. This

138

police state is blessed (if that is the word) by a technology beyond the dreams of the simple agrarian economy of the kingdom to which our radio listener belongs. And what is the news on the radio? It is hard for our listener to make out; his knowledge of the alien language is imperfect, and the static, alas, is heavy. But as far as he can tell, it is a clandestine broadcast—offering the news that a revolt of the people is under way, that both the dictator and the head of the secret police are under arrest. Again, much as in our earlier parable, there is an appeal broadcast for support from the population. Now what is our radio listener to make of this? First he wonders whether he has heard and understood rightly. And then, assuming he has, he finds the same kind of questions crowding into his mind as in the previous story: Is the report genuine, or the deed of a madman, or the clever work of an *agent provocateur*? But the situation is of course more complicated now, because this is not a revolution which directly concerns the kingdom to which our listener belongs, at least not yet. So still further questions arise in his mind: If their revolution is genuine, will it be a help or a hindrance to our own situation? Can we gain help from them for our own struggle, or are our own circumstances so different as to make their struggle meaningless to us? What guidance, if any, can we gain from the static-ridden broadcast signal which I have just heard?

Here, then, is an analogy to our situation with an Old Testament spokesman, and it is really not too pessimistic a picture of the distance between ourselves and the Old Testament material. To a certain degree we *are* eavesdroppers on the old conversation which took place in Jeremiah's lifetime. So how are we to handle the question?

I have titled this chapter "Spokesman Out of Time." I suggest three things. First, that Jeremiah was indeed a spokesman for God in his own time. Second, that he speaks for God out of his own time into ours, and therefore serves as a means by which we may hear God. And third, that in a curious way he may even be said to be *more* at home in our time than in his own.

I shall not take up space here in any attempt to justify my affirmation of the reality of God, or my affirmation of the reality of his dealings with humankind in much the way the biblical material sets him forth, specifically in the way the people of Israel envisaged God and his dealings with them. There is no way for me to prove the validity of the Old Testament witness about God, and I suppose that an agnostic might well make some sense out of the story of Jeremiah as an expression of aberrant psychology (whereby both the "God said" and "I said" of Jeremiah's expression could be understood as conflicting aspects of Jeremiah's conscious mind). To me the risk of accepting the validity, the reality of the vision of Jeremiah and of others in his tradition seems eminently worthwhile, but it is hardly arguable.

At the same time I hasten to add how very keenly aware I am, and how keenly aware we should all be, of the symbolic nature of any talk about God. Thus when I say "God is a person," what I am really saying, I suppose, is that "person" is a more helpful, more adequate description of God than any alternative (to say he is a "process," for example). So to say that Jeremiah's dialogues with that personal God represent a right perception of what is real about God is a highly symbolic way to talk. The Old Testament tradition, however, was equally aware of how distant words are from reality. For example, in the first chapter of Ezekiel, the prophet is attempting to describe the vision he has had of the throne chariot of God, and after an elaborate and picturesque description, he concludes: *"Such* was the *appearance* of the *likeness* of the *glory* of *the Lord* (Ezek. 1:28, italics added)."* Ezekiel is saying, Anything I can say to describe God is a good four steps removed from reality. The Old Testament was thoroughly aware of the symbolic nature of the "God-talk." With this caution, then, I can affirm most heartily that Jeremiah was not mistaken, or demented, in his claim; he really was a spokesman for God in his own generation.

Similarly I can affirm—and again without too much ado—that Jeremiah is a spokesman "out of time," out of his own time into ours. And I do not say this simply because Jeremiah's story is now "in the book," is now scripture, nor because the church or my own tradition tells me that I must believe the story to be relevant to us or truth to us; these are in their way possible reasons for saying yes, but I think there are better ones. I do not say it even because the story fascinates me and may fascinate others to whom the story has been introduced, though that is true too. We could make similar affirmations about the stories of Socrates or Lincoln or Gandhi; we have indicated this already. No, I say it because one can gain through the story of Jeremiah an awareness of being addressed, of being caught up and dealt with in a way that both "breaks down" and "builds," both "plucks up" and "plants," to use once more the terms of Jeremiah's call. One senses that one may become transformed in one's self, and that one's community may become transformed, by material like this. Of course this seems to be a characteristic of biblical material in general, but we are confining our attention now to Jeremiah. This is *why* it has become scripture for the Jewish and Christian communities. It has not become scripture because some synod or council pronounced it so by fiat. It has become scripture because Jeremiah's experience of the word as "fire" continued to be the experience of others as they were exposed to that word; and in this experience we ourselves may share.

We may go further. The phrase "out of time" in our title may be understood rather differently than simply "out of his time into ours," which is what we have been saying up to now. Sometimes we say that a remark is "out of character" or that a picture is "out of focus." I suggest that Jeremiah, the spokesman for God in his own day, was "out of time" in *that* sense; that he not only speaks to us, but speaks to us in an even *more* special and direct way *than to his own time*. This is a new notion for us and one which takes a bit of discussion. How could Jeremiah be more at home with us than with his own generation? This is a strange suggestion, if there is any truth to the parable about eavesdropping which we used just now, if there is truth to our steady affirmation that Jeremiah was not conscious of the far future at all.

But I am not suggesting here that he deliberately spoke to the far future. No person in history ever has the understanding of his own place in history which later times can gain. I am not suggesting that Jeremiah looked to the far future, but rather that he was lonely in his own day for kindred spirits, and that our own generation offers such kindred spirits for him; that there may be ways in which we hear him, and thus hear God through him, more directly than his peers did. I am thus not suggesting that Jeremiah deliberately spoke to the far future, but that God can speak to us in our context more directly than perhaps he was able to do to the folk in Jeremiah's day through those words which Jeremiah spoke.

In what ways might Jeremiah speak to us more than to his own folk? The first way is a way which I fear can only be measured subjectively. We gain the impression, as we become acquainted with Jeremiah in word and deed, that we are in touch here with a person of great poetic skill, a person of innovativeness and daring in his mode of expression, a person of a highly original turn of mind. This impression is hard to illustrate concretely, particularly if we are confined to reading an English translation of the material. We can all recognize that much of the marvel and magic of a poem is lost in translation, and biblical material is no different in this regard. His innovativeness in poetic technique, then, is hard to measure. And, more broadly: How, over the long distance of the centuries and the contrast of cultures, are we to measure "the originality of a mind," whatever that is? But still, subliminally perhaps, the impression comes through to us from Jeremiah's words and works, of an innovator, an independent thinker; it is a trait that appeals to many of us, and more, we suspect, than it appealed to his peers. This trait gives us our own warrant not to squelch any independent and innovative impulses in our thinking and talking about God and his work. We recall the curious visions of the woman embracing the man and of the new covenant to be drawn up by God, in chapter 31 (see chapter VIII). That is the trait we are talking about.

The second way in which Jeremiah may speak to us is in his description of social isolation (recall the discussion in chapter VI). Social isolation, as we have seen, was much rarer in Old Testament times than it is today. In Jeremiah's case it was both exemplified and climaxed in the call to celibacy, a call in which he was unique in the Old Testament. It was a gesture which rendered his whole life inconceivable to his fellows. Here is an aberrant character trait which, whatever its origin may have been psychologically, served in Jeremiah's own mind as the positive vehicle for a message from God.

But it did bring him isolation, terrible isolation.

Now, it is certainly true that what was highly odd in Old Testament times is a commonplace today; our age is crowded with alienated, isolated people. A good many of these people are of course not alienated and isolated in any fashion that strikes us as healthy and helpful, as Jeremiah's does. But at the same time there are a good many other people in our day who are alienated and isolated for what seem to be pretty healthy reasons: alienated

142

from smothering or hostile parental control, or alienated from a culture that thrives on violence and cruelty. These folk may well resonate with the sad, soaring lines of Jeremiah, and here we really do seem to have a point at which Jeremiah meets a modern need in quite a modern way. Other points of view are possible. We might say, for example, that Jeremiah's isolation was unhealthy, or we might say that his stance was creative in his own day but unrelated to our own kinds of alienation, which might be destructive, which might be leading us away from the kind of solidarity which we ought to be building in our own society. We might defend these alternative ways of understanding the issue, but I think what I have set forth is more likely: that Jeremiah's own isolation helps to give resonance to at least some kinds of positive feelings of isolation in our own day.

Closely related to his social isolation is Jeremiah's exploration of the problem of God, the third way in which he may appeal to us more than he did to his own generation. We were struck, in our study of Jeremiah's expressions of bitterness to God, by his astonishing frankness. Let us recall what we learned at the very beginning of chapter I: that Jeremiah is alone, among the prophets of whom we have record, in finding his own relationship to God to be a problem. Amos, so far as we know, simply let his mouth speak the word from God; so Hosea and Isaiah and the rest. The other prophets sensed the two-way struggle between God and the nation and saw themselves the mouthpiece for God in voicing his side of that struggle. Jeremiah, of course, also saw that two-way struggle and likewise voiced God's side of the struggle. But for Jeremiah it became a three-way struggle; God, Jeremiah, and the people were all involved in the argumentation. This is a quantum jump.

One might cite a similar quantum jump out of the tradition of ancient Greece. Greek tragic drama had evolved out of recitations and choral singing which were a part of religious observance, and the great dramatist Aeschylus (? 525-456 B.C.) created tragedies with two actors on the stage at once, alongside the chorus. But the second great tragedian, Sophocles (497/5-406 B.C.), added at times a third actor on the stage: certainly three-way conversations may enhance the dramatic possibilities greatly. [3]

Such was Jeremiah's injection of himself into the arena along

143

with God and the people. God had his bill of complaints against the people, but Jeremiah had his bill of complaints against God. It is getting exciting now, and this is an excitement to which many of us can respond.

The Old Testament scholar Gerhard von Rad has put it well:

[The confessions] all point alike to a darkness which the prophet was powerless to overcome, and this makes them a unity. It is a darkness so terrible—it could also be said that it is something so absolutely new in the dealings between Israel and her God—that it constitutes a menace to very much more than the life of a single man: God's whole way with Israel hereby threatens to end in some kind of metaphysical abyss. For the sufferings here set forth were not just the concern of the man Jeremiah, who here speaks, as it were, unofficially, as a private individual, about experiences common to all men. [4]

Precisely: and the narrow company of those who have embarked upon the exploration of despair before God as to God's ways— that company which began with Jeremiah and with the psalmist who sang, "My God, my God, why hast thou forsaken me?" and continued in Jesus, who repeated the psalm in his own hour of dereliction, through the medieval mystics who described the "dark night of the soul"—has become in our day a much larger company, in a very different context, a context of rationalism, a context of doubt of all God-talk: a company of folk like many of us who cannot find the hand of God so clearly in the world and in our lives but who still, in the name of God, would question his ways and struggle with him. And so to those of us in that situation Jeremiah stands as a pioneer; what seems to have been an oddity in Jeremiah's life has now become much more general for us; and so again, as with his sense of isolation, he does seem more akin to us than to his own contemporaries.

Now our answers so far to the question of how Jeremiah speaks to us in our own day—in his innovativeness, his sense of social isolation, his seeing his relationship to God to be a problem— have focused on Jeremiah. But, we remind ourselves, we are taking seriously his claim to be a *spokesman*, and so we must ask ourselves now what we may learn about *God* from Jeremiah.

Earlier in this chapter we indicated one wrong approach: to

144

apply a word of Jeremiah's to a situation of our own which (at least superficially) seems parallel—in the case of our example, to expect a president of the United States to repent. But if this is wrong, then I suggest it is equally wrong to swing too far in the other direction, in the direction of generalities, of "principles." It will not do, when we try to hear God through Jeremiah, to confine what we learn to platitudes like "God always wants people to be just and righteous" or "God expects us to be in solidarity with our neighbors." One can gain such lessons from almost any page of scripture—indeed, from almost any page of any other moral teacher across the history of mankind. To confine ourselves to such "principles" is to trivialize the specificities of Jeremiah.

What then? There is another solution, one that is obvious and yet quite radical and frightening to many of us. And that is this: the purpose of all scripture, ultimately, and certainly the purpose of the book of Jeremiah for us, I should say, is to lead us to become acquainted with God for ourselves, to enter into our own dialogue with him. The great complaint in Jeremiah 2, we recall, is that the people had turned their back on God; so in our turn we are called to turn our face toward God, to enter into dialogue with him, become involved with him, allow him to show us how we are responsible to him for our common life.

This is obvious, I say, and yet frightening. We would far rather retreat into "principles"—justice or solidarity or peace—than to face the consequences of an obligation to become acquainted with God ourselves.

What the book of Jeremiah offers us, then, is a slice of God's dialogue with his people (and with his prophet) at a particular time in history. By eavesdropping on his dialogue, we can become acquainted with God and become enabled all the more securely to embark upon our own dialogue with God in our own day. The pages of the book of Jeremiah allow us "for instances" of God's reaction to people's lives. And since the lives of the Israelites, though in some ways so very different from our own, are at the same time in other (crucial) ways not so very different after all, we catch some of the cues we need to begin responding to God ourselves.

For example, we saw from the Temple Sermon that God was (at that time) anti-Temple. This does not necessarily mean for us that God is against our own liturgies or the Vatican or the

National Council of Churches or anything else. But what it does mean for us is, God *can* be anti-Temple, and was once, according to Jeremiah 7. How then will God react to our liturgies or to our various religious establishments? The book of Jeremiah urges us to find out.

Again, God declared war on his own people, according to the material in 4:5 and following. This should not mean automatically that God is against his own people today, but it does mean that he *can* be. The question then beckons: Is he now? And such a question leads us all into situations of prayer and discussion which can become part of an ongoing dialogue of listening to God and speaking to God in our own day.

Perhaps the most striking impression we gain from eavesdropping on Jeremiah's presentation of God is the way God is portrayed as being free-lance, as being innovative. That is what bothered Hananiah so. God is constantly changing the agenda. Of course this portrayal of God is not limited to Jeremiah; one finds it in Isaiah—and in Jesus—and at many points in scripture. But it is peculiarly apparent in Jeremiah in his insistence that the time has come for God to write "finis" to the history of his people, at least for the time being.

Some years ago the British scholar J. B. Phillips wrote a little book called *Your God Is Too Small.*[5] His title embodies Jeremiah's message as well: Your God is too small. You thought the God you worshiped has needed the Temple and Zion and Jerusalem and kingship in the line of David and the army of Judah and all the rest. But you are wrong, he doesn't; he is far, far above all these specificities. He does not *need you*, or your religious system, or your notions of state and cult. He does not *need* the whole wide world, even; he is far beyond these little necessities. He constantly has new possibilities up his sleeve, bringing new patterns when the old ones have decayed, bringing new life where there has been only death. Open your ears and listen to him; shake yourself loose from the ways of the past. You can depend on nothing at all in this world, nothing at all in God, even, save one thing only: his steady purpose and his promise to his people.

The question posed to us in our own day, then, by this shaft of light from the past is very simple: Are we up to it? Are we up to such a vision of God which, if followed loyally, would mean a

146

shaking loose from all conventional verities? Are we really up to it?

There is one more problem here, already touched on, of which we must take account before we round off our study, and that is this: Jesus interposes himself between Jeremiah and us—and has Jesus not given us his reassurance in the face of the yawning abyss of Jeremiah's view of God? To be more specific, has Jesus not reassured us that all is well between ourselves and God, so that we no longer need to be threatened by the possibility that God would declare war on his people? After all, did Paul not write:

> We know that in everything God works for good with those who love him, who are called according to his purpose. . . . What then shall we say to this? If God is for us, who is against us? . . . I am sure that neither death, nor life, nor angels, nor principalities, nor things present, nor things to come, nor powers, nor height, nor depth, nor anything else in all creation, will be able to separate us from the love of God in Christ Jesus our Lord.
> —Romans 8:28,31,38-39

Given *this* set of signals, what relevance can those earlier signals from Jeremiah possibly have for us? This is the same question as that asked earlier in this chapter, as to whether the New Testament replaces, supplements, or explains the Old Testament.

Our answer to this question depends somewhat on our taste and tradition. Many Christians will see the image of God's warfare upon his own people as having a once-and-for-all relevance, set aside now in view of the more hopeful perspective of the New Testament. In effect, then, such folk will assume that in this respect at least the New Testament does replace the Old.

Others (and I confess myself to be included here) are not so sure. Perhaps my own approach is exemplified by the statement made by a newspaper editor some years ago, that the task of a newspaper is to comfort the afflicted and to afflict the comfortable. One senses that this was the task of the spokesman for God as well: to afflict the comfortable in times of plenty and complacency (as Jeremiah did before the fall of Jerusalem) and to comfort the afflicted in times of penury and dismay (as Jeremiah evidently did after the fall of Jerusalem).

147

Some folk need one set of messages under one set of conditions, other folk need another set of messages under another set of conditions. Recently I had occasion to offer the same series of class sessions on Jeremiah to members of two different church groups during the same period of time. The first was a church in an outer suburban area of Boston. This congregation shares some of the liveliest and most genuine worship services in which I have ever participated, and out of this congregation thirty or forty men and women came each week to study Jeremiah. The other group which I taught emerged out of a cooperative venture of five neighboring churches of various denominations in an inner-city area near the Boston airport. I was not able to share in the Sunday worship of any of these folk, but certainly the buildings in which they worship, lovingly cared for though they are, are now far too large, and far too much in need of renovation, for the resources of their congregations, and the budgets of several of them are subsidized by their respective denominations. The twenty-odd folk who came to these class sessions were bewildered, baffled people who clung to their neighborhood but who had little sense of being in control of their lives.

The contrast in reaction of the two groups to the story of Jeremiah could hardly have been greater. The suburban church immediately became engrossed in the material and began to raise all sorts of terribly important questions: How does the prophet get his word? How can we be sure we know how to respond ourselves to the word? What are our present-day issues which are clarified by this word from the past? The inner-city folk, on the other hand, were largely mute; defeated to begin with, they hardly had room in their lives for one more tragedy from the past, no matter whether it was "in the book" or not. And I kept asking myself, What am I doing here? Why am I not witnessing to the New Testament gospel to these quiet, puzzled people?

Because, you see, the basic focus of Jeremiah's message is this: You can change the texture of your common life together; turn about, reform your ways with your neighbors, restore your vision of the common welfare, respond to God's call to justice and peace, and perhaps even now he will call off the foe from the north. But to listen in on *this* wavelength implies a certain awareness of control over the life of one's community. And those who do have a certain measure of control over the life of their

148

community, and who do *not* hear the word from Jeremiah and respond to it, have missed part of God's word for our day.

But the folk in the inner city were people who for years had felt largely trapped in their lives. They were only at the beginning stages of recovering any sense of even partial control over the life of their community. (One evening one of their pastors announced, "Tomorrow morning at nine o'clock there will be a public hearing at Faneuil Hall regarding the proposed extension of the runways of Logan Airport. I hope that as many of you as can will be there to show the solidarity on this matter which we all feel in this neighborhood.") These folk sensed, deep down, that their lives had been ruled not by the modern equivalent of King Jehoiakim, who can be addressed by Jeremiah, but rather by the modern equivalent of principalities and powers (once more, Romans 8:38), whom no one can get at; and what they desperately needed to hear is the story that once upon a time, once and for all, God signaled to us that these principalities and powers have no ultimate hold on our poor little lives, if only we quietly say "yes" to God.

Both messages we need; both messages we have. One does not cancel the other, for both of them come from the same God, a God who works within history, and yet works beyond history, and in spite of history, as well.

And so we expand the beachhead of scripture with which we are familiar, moving out beyond the well-used passages of the gospels and epistles and psalms, to listen in on the prophets of old, who had a message for their time that was startling and shocking, a message often thoroughly unwelcome, a message which God expects us, too, to hear. And among these prophets, not the least is Jeremiah.

149

Additional Reading and Resources

The reader who wishes to do further reading on the book of Jeremiah is urged to look into one or both of the following recent commentaries in English: J. Philip Hyatt, *The Interpreter's Bible,* vol. V (New York and Nashville: Abingdon Press, 1956), pp. 777-1142; and John Bright, *Jeremiah [The Anchor Bible]* (Garden City, N.Y.: Doubleday, 1965).

By far the most complete technical commentary on Jeremiah which is presently available is in German: Wilhelm Rudolph, *Jeremia [Handbuch zum Alten Testament]* (Tübingen: J. C. B. Mohr, 1968).

There are many specialized studies which have proved their usefulness. One in particular, John Skinner, *Prophecy and Religion, Studies in the Life of Jeremiah* (New York: Cambridge University Press, 1922; paperback edition, 1961), is well worth reading, though in its critical judgments it is now somewhat out of date.

For the technically minded reader who wishes to consult the more detailed treatments which I have offered elsewhere on various controversial matters dealt with in this book, the following references may be helpful. In them the following abbreviations are used: *JBL: Journal of Biblical Literature*; *VT: Vetus Testamentum*; and *Archit.*: my work *The Architecture of Jeremiah 1-20* (Lewisburg, Pa.: Bucknell University Press, 1974).

Chapter II. The low chronology, and Jeremiah the second Moses: *JBL* 1964, pp. 153-64, and 1966, pp. 17-27; exegesis of 15:16: *JBL* 1966, pp. 21-24; four verbs in 1:10: *JBL* 1960, pp. 363-64.

Chapter III. The general structure of the harlotry material in chapters 2-3: *Archit.*, chap. 3; exegesis of 2:23-24: *VT* 1968, pp. 256-60 (with Kenneth E. Bailey); the verb "turn/return," especially in chapter 3: *The Root Šûbh in the Old Testament* (Leiden: E. J. Brill, 1958), especially pp. 1-3, 116-20, 129-30, 149-53, 156-57.

Chapter IV. The general structure and identification of speakers in the war poetry of Jer. 4—6: *Archit.*, chap. 4, and more particularly for chapter 4, see there sect. g, and for the "prelude" in chapter 4 and the "postlude" in chapter 8, see sects. a, o; the pun in 4:22: *Archit.* 4,f; exegesis of 4:23-26: *JBL* 1966, pp. 404-6, and the *Near East School of Theology Quarterly* (Beirut, Lebanon), vol. 12, no. 1 (Easter, 1964), pp. 2-23; the general structure and identification of speakers in the war poetry of 8:14—10:25: *Archit.* 6, a-f; exegesis of 8:19: *JBL* 1962, pp. 48-49, and *VT* 1962, pp. 494-98; exegesis of 9:3: *Archit.* 6, b, especially note 4 there; exegesis of 9:22: *JBL* 1960, p. 359; exegesis of 10:23-25: *Archit.* 6,e.

Chapter V. The structure of 7:1—8:3 and the location of the material after chapter 6: *Archit.*, chap. 5; prose as a reflection of poetry: *JBL* 1960, pp. 351-67; Jeremiah's dictation of a scroll under the stimulation of the prior discovery of the law scroll in Josiah's reign: *JBL* 1966, p. 26; the suggested identity of the contents of the two scrolls: *Archit.* 10,b.

Chapter VI. Exegesis of 15:17: *Andover Newton Quarterly*, vol. 13, no. 2 (Nov. 1972), pp. 126-27.

Chapter VII. The structure and exegesis of 16:1-9: *JBL* 1966, pp. 412-20; the structure of Jeremiah's complaints against God: *Archit.* 7, a-d, h-i; poetic core to 11:22-23 : *Archit.* 7,d; exegesis of 12:1: *JBL* 1962, pp. 49-51, and *Interpretation*, 1963, pp. 280-87; exegesis of 15:11-12: *Archit.* 7,d; "turn/return" in 15:19: *The Root Šûbh...*, p. 131, and *Archit.* 7,d; exegesis of 17:5-8: *JBL* 1962, p. 52, and *Archit.* 7,i; exegesis of 20:13: *JBL* 1962, pp. 52-53.

Chapter VIII. Exegesis of 30:5-7: *JBL* 1962, pp. 53-54; exegesis of 31:22b: *VT* 1966, pp. 236-39, and *Andover Newton Quarterly*, vol. 12, no. 4 (March 1972), pp. 213-22.

Chapter X. The seeming modernity of Jeremiah and its consequences for our interpretive task: *Andover Newton Quarterly*, vol. 13, no. 2 (Nov. 1972), pp. 115-32.

Notes

Foreword

1. The lectures (called simply *Jeremiah*) were privately printed by the American Mission Press, Istanbul, 1966.

2. *The Works of John Robinson, with a Memoir and Annotations by Robert Ashton* (London: John Snow, 1851), vol. I, p. xliv.

CHAPTER II: THE PROPHET LIKE MOSES

1. The evidence is a bit uncertain but is perhaps to be pieced together from the data in 1 Samuel 2:27-36, 14:3, 22:18-23 and 2 Samuel 8:17. The whole matter is discussed briefly in R. W. Corney, "Abiathar," in *The Interpreter's Dictionary of the Bible* (Nashville: Abingdon Press, 1962), vol. I, pp. 6-7, and, by the same author, "Eli," in the same work, vol. II, p. 85; compare John Bright, *Jeremiah* [*The Anchor Bible*] (New York: Doubleday, 1965), pp. lxxxvii-lxxxviii.

2. For an old tradition about the Ark of the Covenant in Moses' day, see Numbers 10:35-36.

3. The only scholar who has written for the general public who disagrees with the traditional chronology, and who comes to a solution similar to that here proposed, is J. Philip Hyatt; see his introduction and exegesis on Jeremiah in *The Interpreter's Bible*, vol. V (New York: Abingdon Press, 1956), pp. 779-80, 797-98.

4. For a study of this matter, see Stanley B. Frost, "The Death of Josiah, A Conspiracy of Silence," *Journal of Biblical Literature,* LXXXVII (1968), pp. 369-82.

5. See W. Eugene Claburn, "The Fiscal Basis of Josiah's Reforms," *Journal of Biblical Literature,* xcii (1973), pp. 11-22.

6. Herodotus, *Persian Wars,* I, 103-6.

7. For the assumption that the phrase "thy words were found" refers to the reception of the divine word by the prophet, see the German commentary by Artur Weiser, *Das Buch Jeremia* (Göttingen: Vandenhoeck & Ruprecht, 1969), p. 133. Among those who express uneasiness at the phrase is the German scholar F. Giesebrecht in *Das Buch Jeremia* (Gottingen: Vandenhoeck & Ruprecht, 1907), p. 92, who

calls it "a somewhat drastic expression." The American scholar J. Philip Hyatt follows the Greek text; see his commentary (and compare preceding note 3), p. 942, where he cites earlier commentators who choose the same solution.

8. P. R. Reid, *The Colditz Story* (London: Hodder & Stoughton, 1952), chapter XVII.

9. I owe this suggestion to Sheldon H. Blank, *Jeremiah, Man and Prophet* (Cincinnati: Hebrew Union College Press, 1961), pp. 28-29.

CHAPTER III: GOD'S PEOPLE TURN THEIR BACKS

1. Among those who have excised the lines about the wild ass: F. Giesebrecht (see note 7 in chapter II); P. Volz, *Der Prophet Jeremia* (Leipzig: A. Deichertsche Verlagsbuchhandlung, 1928); W. Rudolph, *Jeremia* (Tübingen: J. C. B. Mohr, 1968); A. Weiser (see note 7 in chapter II); and, in English: J. Bright (see note 1 in chapter II).

2. This is the suggestion of J. Philip Hyatt in *The Interpreter's Bible,* vol. V (New York: Abingdon Press, 1956), p. 820.

3. So Bright (see note 1, chapter II).

4. So again Bright.

5. The best general one is perhaps J. Philip Hyatt in *The Interpreter's Bible*, but there are others, for example, Guy P. Courtier, "Jeremiah," in Raymond E. Brown and others, *The Jerome Biblical Commentary* (Englewood Cliffs, N.J.: Prentice-Hall, 1968); in this work the discussion of the additions to chapter 3 is on p. 307.

CHAPTER IV: GOD DECLARES WAR ON HIS PEOPLE

1. Compare Denis Baly, *The Geography of the Bible* (New York: Harper & Brothers, 1957), p. 68; rev. ed. (New York: Harper & Row, 1974), p. 52.

2. The extent of the "postlude" postulated here is not altogether certain, but this verse selection is quite plausible.

3. George Orwell, *Animal Farm* (New York: Harcourt Brace & Co., 1954).

CHAPTER V: A SERMON, A SCROLL, AND A SCRIBE

1. I am well aware that the historical accuracy of this tradition is disputed by some scholars, but my point here is that the *tradition* of Isaiah's conviction of Jerusalem's inviolability was alive and well in Jeremiah's day. For some discussion of the complicated arguments for or against the authenticity of this tradition to Isaiah, see Brevard S. Childs, *Isaiah and the Assyrian Crisis* [*Studies in Biblical Theology,* Second

Series, No. 3] (Naperville, Ill.: Aloe R. Allenson, 1967), and John Bright, *A History of Israel* (Philadelphia: Westminster Press, 2d ed., 1972), pp. 291, 306-8.

2. See note 4, chapter II.

3. The curious wording in Isaiah 8:16 hardly counts; the meaning of the text there is uncertain.

4. See G. Ernest Wright in *The Interpreter's Bible*, vol. II (New York: Abingdon-Cokesbury Press, 1953), p. 326.

5. Our curiosity is of course aroused as to what, precisely, were the contents of the scroll which Jeremiah dictated to Baruch—or, more precisely, what the contents of the two scrolls were, for his second dictation contained all the words of the first, with additions. Many guesses have been made through the years (for Hyatt's guess, for example, see *The Interpreter's Bible*, vol. V, pp. 787-88), but such suggestions have seemed rather subjective, and many commentators have abandoned the problem as insoluble.

I have done some recent study which leads me to suspect that the book of Jeremiah seems to have a rather careful structure to it, and that this structure might even offer a fairly substantial clue as to what the contents of the scrolls might be (though the interested reader may feel that the suggestion which I am giving is just as subjective as were those of earlier scholars!).

Let us review what we can learn from chapter 36 itself. The utterances which were recorded in the scroll were utterances of judgment, for they were intended to lead people to change their ways (verse 7). It is evidently a fairly extensive collection, containing several multiples of three or four columns of writing (verse 23). And what was dictated had a structure in Jeremiah's mind, since he certainly was not willing to risk forgetting any words from God and since he dictated the entire contents a second time (verses 28, 32) along with further material.

Some detective work can lead us at least tentatively to our goal. I suggest that the first scroll contained the call of Jeremiah (1:4-10) and possibly the two visions (1:11-14) as well. Now a central word in that call was "youth." And chapter 2 begins with a poem containing "youth" (2:2), so that the words of the call are locked in to the first poem in chapter 2. Now the synonym for "youth" in 2:2 is "bride," and the last poem in chapter 2 (2:29-37) has at its midpoint the word "bride" once more. And then the material in chapter 3 begins and ends with "youth" (3:4, 24). In short, the first part of the opening poem, 2:2, maps out, as it were, the shape of the two chapters of the cycle of poems on the harlotry of the nation (that is, the poems in chapter 2 from verse 5 on, and the poems in chapter 3).

Then, as we have seen, the cycle of war poems is locked on to chapter 3 by its prelude (4:1-4) and postlude (8:4-10a and 13), which contain the verb "(re)turn," and the cycle of war poems consisted, as we saw, of seven sections with a symmetry of arrangement:

battle scenes, 4:5-31

the battle that turns to wisdom, 5:1-9 (with refrain)

metaphor of the vineyard Israel, 5:10-17

the lecture of God the schoolmaster, 5:19-29 (with refrain)

battle scenes, 6:1-8

metaphor of the vineyard Israel, 6:9-15

the battle that turns to wisdom, 6:16-26, with the final examination, 6:27-30

In other words, these sections are in the form A-B-C-D-A-C-B. This kind of scheme should be easy to remember. I suggest that this material made up the first dictated scroll, the one which Jehoiakim destroyed.

The second scroll consisted of the contents of the first, plus "many similar words" (36:32). This description would fit the additional three sections added to the cycle of war poems (8:14—9:9, with refrain; 9:17-22; 10:17-25).

Now the material in chapter 11 and beyond in the book of Jeremiah is of a different sort; chapter 11 begins with a long prose passage about obeying the covenant, a passage which appears to have been added to the collection much later, and then (in 11:18) we begin the so-called "confessions," private laments of Jeremiah to God. There is a whole series of these, and we shall study them in chapter VII. Interspersed among all these are many "orphan" units of material which give evidence of having been filed in with existing material on a basis similar to the word association which we spotted as the pretext for the insertion of 7:1—8:3 at its place. In short, nothing else later on in the book of Jeremiah fits the description of chapter 36 so well, and I would suggest that we really may have in these early cycles of material, which we have already studied, the body of words which made up those first dictated collections.

CHAPTER VI: THE PEOPLE AGAINST JEREMIAH

1. See John Bright, *A History of Israel* (Philadelphia: Westminster Press, 2d ed., 1972), p. 326.

2. So Bright, p. 329.

CHAPTER VII: JEREMIAH AGAINST GOD

1. For a thorough study of the whole matter, see George E. Mendenhall, *The Tenth Generation* (Baltimore: Johns Hopkins Press, 1973), chapter III, "The Vengeance of Yahweh," especially p. 97.

2. See William R. Taylor in *The Interpreter's Bible*, vol. IV (New

York: Abingdon Press, 1955), p. 18, on Psalm 1, and J. Philip Hyatt in *The Interpreter's Bible*, vol. V (New York: Abingdon Press, 1956), pp. 950-51, on Jeremiah 17:5-8.

3. Compare the suggestions of Hyatt in *The Interpreter's Bible*, vol. V, pp. 939-40.

4. *Hamlet*, I, iii.

5. See Samuel Terrien in *The Interpreter's Bible*, vol. III (New York: Abingdon Press, 1954), pp. 888-90.

6. See further, H. Wheeler Robinson, *The Cross in the Old Testament* (London: S. C. M. Press, 1955).

CHAPTER VIII: TO BUILD AND TO PLANT

1. *Time*, Sept. 28, 1970, p. 17.

2. Many commentators assume that the greater part of the material in chapters 30-31 was originally intended for the north, but this seems to be an unnecessary assumption. Compare the discussion in John Bright, *Jeremiah [The Anchor Bible]* (New York: Doubleday, 1965), pp. 284-85.

3. Compare John Bright, *Jeremiah [The Anchor Bible]*, p. 32.

4. W. F. Albright, "An Ostracon from Calah and the North Israelite Diaspora," *Bulletin of the American Schools of Oriental Research,* #149 (Feb. 1958), pp. 33-36.

5. See *Newsweek*, Feb. 23, 1970, p. 86.

6. In a work of the Dead Sea community which has been given a variety of titles and reference numbers. In R. H. Charles, *The Apocrypha and Pseudepigrapha of the Old Testament* (Oxford: Clarendon Press, 1913), vol. II, the work was called "Fragments of a Zadokite Work," and the passage is found at 8:15 (p. 814). In a more recent edition, Geza Vermes, *The Dead Sea Scrolls in English* (Baltimore: Penguin Books, rev. ed., 1968), the work is titled "The Damascus Rule," and the passage is found on p. 103. The technical abbreviation for the work among scholars is now *CD*, and the citation (by column and line) is vi 19. It is further to be noted that there are other passages in the Dead Sea Scrolls which offer similar wording, but this is perhaps the clearest reference.

CHAPTER IX: JEREMIAH BEYOND JUDAH

1. W.F. Albright argues for a date in the mid-seventh century B.C., in a review in *Journal of Biblical Literature*, LXI (1942), p. 119.

2. For reference to this legend, see *The Jewish Encyclopedia* (New York: Funk and Wagnalls, 1901-6), vol. VII, p. 102a.

3. For the whole idea of the book of Jeremiah as a memorial, see Stanley B. Frost, "The Memorial of the Childless Man, A Study in

Hebrew Thought on Immortality," *Interpretation*, XXVI (1972), pp. 446-47.

CHAPTER X: SPOKESMAN OUT OF TIME

1. Phyllis Trible, "Ancient Priests and Modern Polluters," *Andover Newton Quarterly*, Nov. 1971, p. 75.
2. Oscar Cullman, *Christ and Time* (Philadelphia: Westminster Press, 1950), p. 84. The italics are his.
3. For a discussion of this matter, see H. D. F. Kitto, "Sophocles," in *Encyclopedia Britannica* (1970), vol. 20, p. 918a. The interested reader may look up Kitto's illustration, the messenger scene in Sophocles' *Electra*, found at lines 673-79.
4. Gerhard von Rad, *Old Testament Theology* (New York: Harper & Row, 1965), vol. II, p. 204, reprinted in *The Message of the Prophets* (New York: Harper & Row, 1972), pp. 173-74.
5. J. B. Phillips, *Your God Is Too Small* (New York: Macmillan, 1953).